Norma Dolby's Diary

An Account of the Great Miners' Strike

VERSO

The imprint of New Left Books

First published 1987
© Norma Dolby 1987

Verso
6 Meard Street, London W1

Typeset in Parlament by
Leaper & Gard Ltd, Bristol

Printed in Great Britain by
Thetford Press Limited, Thetford, Norfolk

British Library
Cataloguing in Publication Data

Dolby, Norma
    Norma Dolby's diary.
    1. Coal-miners—Great Britain
    I. Title
    331.89'2822334'0924   HD8039-M62G7

    ISBN 0-86091-169-1
    ISBN 0-86091-880-7 Pbk

Acknowledgements

My initial thanks to Marion, Hilary, Leo, Geoff, Brian, and Paul, who gave me their friendship and expressed their confidence in my book. Their support helped me greatly when there were times that I felt like giving up.

My thanks also to the publishers, for having faith in my book.

I dedicate this book to my husband Terry, and all my family and friends, who stood by me when things got really rough. Also to all our comrades and friends who have lost their jobs, or are still in prison.

March 1984

March 12, 1984. A day I will never forget. The scars it has left on my brain will always remain with me. For many more people as well, life would never be the same again.

It started just like any other Monday — very dreary, with plenty of chores to get through — but it was to turn into a nightmare. This was the day that the Yorkshire pickets descended on our Derbyshire pits just like a plague of locusts.

I am just an ordinary miner's wife. My name is Norma Dolby. I live with my husband Terry, and three children, who are all boys, in a little terraced house in a small mining village called Arkwright Town. You can be forgiven if you have never heard of it, as it is made up of just five rows of houses, a few pensioners' bungalows, and four council houses. We have a saying in Arkwright that if you blink an eye, passing through in a car, you would miss the village completely. Mind you, we can boast of having a public house, Miners Welfare, Community School, St John's Ambulance Hut, as well as three shops. At this stage I should point out that my friends and I are not really alcoholics, even though I have put the public house first, though I must admit that many a time I felt like turning to the demon drink.

Arkwright is a very close-knit community. Everyone knows each other. Before you are accepted here you have to live in the village a few years. Generations of families live here. You have to think twice before you say anything about anyone, as it always gets back to them. To be fair, people are on the whole very friendly in the village. To get to our pit, we have to go down a very steep hill, so when our men come out of the pit, after a gruelling shift, they have to have many a breather to get back up the hill.

Already we know that our pit is doomed. It will shut down in 1989, if not sooner. We are now down to 540 men working the pit. My Terry is one of them. The rest have either been made redundant, or transferred to other local pits. Never will I forget the day that we heard rumours of a National Strike. My stomach still turns over at the thought of it. We already know that our pit is to shut, so our men are very bitter about coming out. Nobody was bothered about us, so why should we bother about Yorkshire? We have nothing to gain by striking, and besides, we in Derbyshire voted to work. So work we will, until we have a national ballot.

Of course, it was a case of famous last words. We heard on the news that the Yorkshire pickets were on their way to Derbyshire to close all the pits. My heart nearly stopped beating. Surely they would not come to our pit. With being on the overtime ban since November, we were already deep in debt. I tried to reassure myself. It would not happen to us. They would not find our pit. It is only small, and out of the way. That is how crazy and mixed up I was, completely forgetting that the Yorkshire pickets would have been given the lists of pits in the area and maps to find them.

Terry was on nightshift. Waiting for him to go to work that terrible night, I felt drained of all emotion. What if they were already there and he got hurt? I kept watching the clock. Now it was time for Terry to go. I could not stand it any longer. My legs felt like jelly. 'Can I come with you?' I said. 'Don't be silly. I would feel a proper fool, letting you go down with me. I can take care of myself,' he replied.

After Terry had gone, I just broke down and sobbed my heart out. I felt so alone at that moment. Little did I know that I would be shedding tears for months to come. That night seemed like an eternity. At last, there was a key in the lock, and yes it was Terry back. I rushed down the stairs, 'What happened? Were they there? Did they try to stop you?' I asked him.

10

'Calm down, and stop worrying. Everything was nice and peaceful,' Terry replied. 'I have heard that the Yorkshire pickets are coming tomorrow, but I am going through them. We have not voted to strike.'

Thank God, I thought, but it still did not stop me from worrying for the rest of the day. Terry had gone to bed. I kept wanting to wake him up. I could not stand the pressure. I just wanted Terry to hold me in his arms, and reassure me that everything would be alright. Finally I could stand it no longer, I just had to get out of the house. All my nerves were on edge, I had to speak to someone. My thoughts were in complete turmoil.

I rushed down to my friend Ann's house. She looked very calm as I poured out all my worries to her. 'Don't worry so much. If it happens, we will manage somehow. We will all be in the same boat,' Ann said to me.

She put the kettle on while we were sat talking. Her son, Adrian, came in, and he seemed very upset. 'Yorkshire pickets have come and stopped us going into work,' he said.

I looked at Ann. How dare they do this to us. It can not be true. Oh, please God let me be dreaming. But I knew deep down it was no dream. This was reality.

By the time I got back home, Terry had got up. He kept repeating, 'Don't worry love, everything will be alright,' but he must have known it was a waste of breath. Even I know that I am a born whittler.

The night dragged on, until it was time for Terry to go to work once again. 'Be careful,' I told him, but you know what men are like. He just turned round and said, 'I am capable of looking after myself. I have got my key, so just lock the door and go to bed.'

After he had gone, I wanted to creep out to see what was happening. But, as the whole village was swarming with police, I quickly shut the door. The next hour was really agony. It was the not knowing what was happening that made it worse. I felt as if I could not breathe, and every time I heard a noise, my stomach kept doing double somersaults.

Suddenly, my waiting was over. Terry was coming through the door. Oh how I thanked God that he was safe, but I was ashamed at the same time. My heart sank. The worst had happened. The men had been prevented from going in to work.

Terry explained that the Union officials at Chesterfield had met them at the pit gates and advised the men to stop out on strike so that there would be no unpleasantness with the Yorkshire men.

We tossed and turned that night. We just couldn't get to sleep. All I could think about was my family. What would happen to our poor children? What was to become of them? Terry is a person who never shows his feelings, but I could see that he was worrying too, as he was too quiet. I know, it could not have helped him with me going on about everything.

The following day, the men from Arkwright pit had a meeting with their Union officials to decide what course of action to take next. I could not rest in the house on my own, so down I went again to Ann's house. My three other friends, Helen, Una, and Pam, were already there, discussing all the events that had happened. Ann made us a cup of tea, as we sat and chatted, but we were all naturally very worried, so between us we were a bright shower. At least we did come up with a really marvellous idea. If we all bought a sack of potatoes, a tray of eggs and a few loaves of bread for the freezer, we would not starve, or so we thought. When I look back on the strike, I realise that the girls always cheered me up. Sometimes, I wonder how I would have got through those first couple of months without their help. I had really good friends, for which I will always be grateful.

So this is it then. We are now officially on strike. Terry has just come in and said that they will be picketing their own pit in future. I will just have to resign myself to the fact. We will have to get on with it. I was sure at that time that it would last only a couple of weeks. Maybe it was as well that I did not know just how long it would last, as I am sure I would have had a mental breakdown.

I was lucky to have a part-time job, at our Miners' Welfare, at least I thought that at the time.

Then one day Terry came back from a meeting at the Club, telling me that it was to be our Strike Centre. Little did I know just how this would affect me, but I was to very soon find out.

The very next day three of us ladies from the village set off to go to work at the Club. We had to start at nine o'clock, but when we arrived at the top of our street there were pickets and police everywhere. Talk about being royalty! We were given a police escort right to the Club doors. Mind you, after second thoughts, they did not look that friendly really. Was this sleepy little Arkwright, with police vans on every corner? It looked more like a scene from a gangster film. Normally, all that ever happens in Arkwright is births, deaths, marriages, and of course the occasional couple running off together, but that is another story altogether.

When we did finally get into the club, we just could not believe our eyes. It looked just like a betting shop. Men were sprawled out everywhere, plastic cups were littered all over the place, and sat among all this, was our Union man, paying the men their picketing money and dividing them into three groups, for mornings, afternoons, and nights. Most of the village men were to do the nights, so as to cut out a lot of the travelling. Of course a lot of men on strike never did one shift of picketing. They were content to stay at home until it was all over.

How we got the club clean that day I will never know. We had a right good laugh when we were cleaning the men's toilet. Some of them walked in and I do not know whose face was more brightly coloured. You know what men are like, unzipping on the way in. It ended up with us ladies coming out of the toilets, and shouting to the men, 'You have got five minutes, then we are locking the doors.' Talk about a stampede, we were nearly knocked down in the rush. After that we used to stand by the door, shouting, 'Is there anybody there?' Talk about feeling an idiot!

In these early days of the strike, our son Jonathan and his friend Paul, who were only ten years old at that time, used to go picketing with their dads. All the men made a great fuss of them, even to sharing their snap with them, and of course learning them cheeky jokes, and to shout scab at the under-manager, who was good with the men, so he used to laugh at them. At this time, the men were solid at the pit. Only the deputies and cleaning ladies were going into work. They did not mind them going into work as they were in a different union anyway, so there were no clashes with the police at this time. It was just a shame that the police felt it necessary to be there. Perhaps many of the terrible things that were to happen later would never have been if it was not for the police presence.

How many miners have died for what they believe in! I, like many more, will never forget how young David Jones lost the right to live on the very first picketing he did. We were all numb with shock when we heard it on the television. Our hearts bled for his family. How would they get over their tragic loss? They never found out what caused his fatal injury. Rightly the court passed an open verdict. David was buried on March 23rd. All our love and prayers were with you that day and always will be, Doreen and Mark, David's mother and father. I just pray that one day justice will be done.

David's death of course was the first of many. We lost Joe Green later on, in tragic circumstances, and we were to learn of a lot more deaths before the year was out, and thousands injured on the picket lines. It should never have happened in our country. It never failed to amaze me; just where did all the police come from? I had never seen so many before in all my life.

May 1984

It was in May that I realized that I wanted to get more involved with the strike. Ann, Una, and myself were asked by Audrey Bagshaw if we would like to help with the food parcels. We were all very willing so we set up a committee. Audrey was to be Chairwoman; I was to be Treasurer; Ann and Una would go to the local supermarket each week to buy in the extra food. Harriet, who had retired from the pit canteen, also joined our committee. She would do a raffle for us each week to bring in extra money. We were receiving ninety parcels a week from Chesterfield Centre, each worth about £1.50. At this time we had to make up another fifty parcels, and later it was to get even worse. Finding the extra money was to prove a right headache.

Someone came up with the brilliant idea of holding a jumble sale. Soon you could not get into our house for jumble; our front room was stacked high. Terry kept getting his hair off, but I could not blame him, as you had to sit on top of sacks to watch television. (I suppose we were very lucky to still have a television, as a lot of poor families had to send them back.) I am happy to say that our jumble sale was a huge success. The lads did not have a lot of money to spend, but for a little while it took their minds off the strike. We had advertised it well, so lots of people from surrounding villages joined in. I had made a cake in the shape of a violin for the raffle. Whoever had the winning ticket must have thrown it away, or lost it, as the cake was not claimed; after two days, we cut it up for the lads, and they really enjoyed it with a cup of tea. We

15

were all very tired after the jumble sale, but also very happy, as we raised one hundred and six pounds. This would buy parcels for another two weeks.

It was in May that I decided to give up my job, and give all my time and energy to helping the lads. They now needed our support more than ever. It would not have been so bad if we could have seen just a glimmer of light at the end of the tunnel, but at this time there was nothing to look forward to at all. We were very fortunate to have some very good friends from Haversage and Bradwell in Derbyshire, who would come to our Centre every few weeks, bringing us boxes of food, some clothes, and a little money. Never once did they falter in their support for us, and always cheered us up whenever we felt down in the dumps. Little did we know just how much they were to help us in future months.

It was mostly Janet and Beryl that bought us the food. We used to sort out all the little luxuries, like coffee and tea and tinned meat, to put in the weekly raffle. We made it into a food hamper — at least that's what we liked to call it — really it was just a few items in a wire basket. But it was a big occasion when it was drawn, with everyone willing their ticket to come out. We let different lads give the drum with the tickets a twirl, then someone would draw the winning ticket out. It was lovely whenever a single lad won it, and more often than not he would share it with one of his mates. That day, they would go home happy, and we also would be happy, knowing that we now had some more money to buy food for the following week.

We were putting up more parcels than ever now. No one was refused a parcel, as everyone was in the same boat, struggling for survival. The lads had from Monday until Friday to put their names down for a parcel. This was to give us some idea how many to put up. We were doing at least two hundred a week. We gave them out on a Thursday morning, ticking off the names as we passed them over. At last we had some good news. Derbyshire County Council was to give every miner's family thirty pounds to buy extras with. Everyone was talking about it. After all, it was a great sum of money, and we all rushed

16

to fill a form in, and send it off to them, hoping and praying that it would not take them very long to send the money. Our prayers were answered within the week. I was very excited when I ripped open the letter. Thirty pounds! What a fortune! I hugged the cheque to me, and laughed out loud, while doing a little dance all around the kitchen. If anyone could have seen me they would have thought that I had flipped my lid. I could not wait to go down town to fill my pantry shelves up again. The thrill of actually being able to look around the shops was fantastic. The girls and I all agreed that I should write and thank the Council, for their wonderful gesture. Yes, the world was full of wonderful people.

Talking about wonderful people, I will never forget how I came to get in contact with another dear friend who lives in London. His name is David Townsend. He is a Director of Social Services. David rang up our strike centre one Monday morning. He belonged to a group called Deptford Fabian Society. They would like to adopt our pit. I often smile at the thought of that conversation. The line was dreadful, buzzing and crackling, and I felt a complete idiot, stuttering and stammering in a panic. Here was someone willing to help us, and I could not understand a word he was saying. He must have thought me a proper fool! But David was so understanding; he said he would ring me later at home. When he did ring me later, he told me that their group would be in touch with us very soon, and within a few days they had sent us a cheque for £50. We were now alright for another week's food.

David explained later that as he had roots in Derbyshire and Yorkshire his group had decided to pick a pit in that area. We were the first pit on the list, so they picked us. God must have been looking down on us that day. Whenever we were in trouble, or needed anything, they were there. Never will these ties be broken; we will be friends for life. There will always be a welcome in my home for David, and any of his family or friends.

One day when we were at the Strike Centre, we had a phone call from Shirebrook. Could as many women as possible get to their pit, as they were having a lot of trouble with the police. We arranged a lift straight away.

Five of us went. When we were stopped by the police at the edge of the village, we acted very innocent, pretending that we were going to visit friends for a coffee morning party. I am sure that the police were not fooled for one moment. I dared not look at them. My heart was pounding in my chest. Surely they could hear it? At last they let us through, and we were on our way again with a few little hysterical giggles, as the police followed us up into the village.

The ladies were waiting for us. They were very upset as the local chimney sweep had just been arrested — along with his five year old son. The poor little lad was crying his eyes out. You might be asking yourselves, what had a chimney sweep to do with a miners' strike? His crime was to tell the police that it was his business where he was going! Surely we were now living in a police state. I wished my heart would behave itself, as here it was again beating a drum inside me. The police refused to let us stand on the pavements. We were all herded into people's gardens. Standing beside me was a young mother, very upset and crying, as she had been separated from her small child. She was pleading with the police: please can I go for my baby? But they refused to let her go. I could not believe my ears. Surely they could not stop her? The child was only about two years old; it was playing further down the street. But here were the police joining arms to stop her passing. I really felt hatred for them at that moment. One of the ladies had the presence of mind to shout to a young boy on a bike to go for the child. What a relief when the baby was handed over to its mother. Surely even the police could not have failed to be moved, when they saw this sobbing young mother hug her baby to her. I had to turn away, as I felt that emotional, and the police would have loved knowing that they could get through to you. We stood huddled together there for at least an hour. I was not used to this treatment. We might have been animals for all the police cared.

The Shirebrook ladies suddenly realized that the bus carrying the scabs had been diverted. Someone shouted, 'the scabs are coming down the back alley', and everyone flew across the gardens. I really felt sorry for the owners

of the gardens, as in the heat of the moment, some of the
ladies got carried away, and trampled all over their plants.
I got caught up with the rush. How I ever got over the big
gate, I will never know. I must have been pushed over.
Now we were running down this alleyway. I was panting
and puffing, and on top of that, I had to go and lose a
shoe. Suddenly we came face to face with two scabs surrounded by police. All hell broke loose. Everyone was
shouting at each other. The police quickly ushered the
men into a nearby house, and that was that. Everyone
started to walk away. You could not believe how quiet it
now was; had it really happened? I felt as if I had just run
a marathon race.

That's it now, until tonight,' the Shirebrook ladies said.
I remember how surprised I was at how calmly they took
it all. It was just a way of life to them. They had scabs
right through the strike. At our pit we were solid for
several months, thank goodness.

June 1984

After nearly three months on strike, we were preparing for big rallies all over the country. We would not be forgotten; we were proud of what we were doing. We wanted everyone to stand alongside us and fight for their rights.

All the rallies were important in their own way, but one I will never forget was when we went to Wigan. The day was red hot, the town was packed with shoppers, and we had a brass band leading us through. Then the police made us go round the outskirts of town, so we seemed to be walking for hours. The sweat was dripping off us; there were hills everywhere; to make matters worse, the strap on my sandal kept slipping off. I was hobbling, trying to pull it up at the same time as marching. But like most of our marches it was made worth while by the people who came out to wave to us, and groups with banners pledging their support. I always felt a lump in my throat at these times.

At last we arrived at the Labour Hall. Inside, it was packed with people waiting to be served with a cool drink. The air was stifling; it hurt to breathe. I was beginning to feel terrible; the lasses made me sit down, while they fetched the drinks. We took them into the main room to listen to the talks, but even this room was packed solid, and some of the lads stood up to let us sit down. (One said afterwards he thought that I was going to pass out, as I looked that bad.) At that moment, I would have done anything to have been home in my cosy bed. But I am pleased to say the talks were well worth going for. They really built me up to face another day in our battle, and more important still, helped me to build up those not fortunate enough to be there. I think that we were all beginning to realize that this strike was not going to disappear overnight. It was now political, and it would be a fight to the finish. So you can see how important these rallies were to us. During the strike, I was to go on five rallies: twice to London, then to Barnsley, Durham, and of course Wigan. Only once did Terry go with me, to Durham, and what a rally that was! The procession stretched for miles. It was a beautiful day. We sat on the banks of the river, eating chips. It was so peaceful there; a far cry from all the stress of the picket line. Arthur Scargill and Neil Kinnock were the main speakers that day, but we did not get to hear Mr Kinnock talk, as we had to make our way back to the bus at two o'clock. On police orders most of the shops were boarded up, only one or two cafes were open, and not one public house. The police were making sure that our lads did not get hold of any drinks.

There was not a lot happening this month. Every week seemed the same. We were just listening to every news bulletin, and wishing for some sign of peace. So it was with some interest that we heard from the union that we had to collect all the names of children who were over thirteen years and put them in a hat. Whoever was drawn out would go on a holiday to France, sponsored by the French miners. My two children's names, Andrew and Shaun, went in the draw. Only about ten names from Arkwright were put down, as some children were not very keen to go all that way without their parents. Our club stewardess, Fay, drew the name out of the hat. What a lovely surprise when our son Shaun's name came out. He would not be going until July, but it left us with the terrible headache of having to fit him up with clothes, as he was now badly in need of them. Terry went to the union and borrowed twenty-five pounds. This helped a little bit. Shaun was not really overjoyed when he heard that he was going. Although he was fifteen, he had never been away on his own before. For the next month, he took a lot of coaxing from us.

July 1984

July was a very busy time for me, what with doing food parcels and also trying to get everything prepared for Shaun's trip to France. I was now having second thoughts about him going. France seemed so very far away, and you hear such terrible things happening to children these days. But there again, I am sure that the French miners will take good care of them. Shaun and another boy, from Yorkshire, are to stop with a French family, who have six children of their own. The day arrived for Shaun to go. Terry and I took him down to Chesterfield, where they were being picked up. Thirteen children were going from our area and they all looked a little worried. It seemed ages before the bus arrived. By this time, I had a lump in my throat, but no way dare I let Shaun see me upset, as it always embarrasses him, more so when all the other children are watching. Now it was time for them all to get on the bus. One young girl started to cry her eyes out. It was a worrying time for her parents, getting her calmed down and onto the bus. As the bus finally moved off, tears came to my eyes. All the children were waving and cheering. The two accompanying adults encouraged them to do this, and we knew then that our children were in good hands. Altogether, forty-three children went, with two adults, and two drivers. After an overnight stop at Canterbury, they travelled on to Dover to catch the 8 am ferry taking them to France. When we got back home, I could not rest. The night seemed to drag on for an eternity. I was pleased when daylight finally came so I could get up to the Strike Centre and keep myself busy.

Every dinner-time the lads in the club used to put the television on, so we could see how the strike was going. What a shock I got, as there was our Shaun waving away on the ferry. It was a lovely change for the media to show a nice side of the strike. Needless to say, that day I was glued to the television for every news.

It turned out a wonderful holiday for Shaun. Everyone was marvellous to them all. Madame Le-Roy, who Shaun stopped with, was a wonderful lady. She insisted on the lads phoning home when ever they felt like it, but I told Shaun only to do so in emergencies. It was a good job that I did not know that Shaun ripped his leg open, while larking about with a young French lass on the top of a bus. He had to have five stitches in it. I was pleased that he was insured. Madame Le-Roy sent us a lovely plate with their pit emblem painted on it. It has pride of place on our display unit. I wish that one day I could meet this very kind and generous family, to thank them personally for all the love and kindness shown towards our children.

We now began to feel a different atmosphere in the village. There was a lot of restlessness as it was suddenly dawning on everyone that we were getting no nearer the end of the strike. Everyone seemed to be watching each other, wondering who would be the first to try to go back to work. Then one day it happened. A woman called Pauline, who worked in the Manager's office, decided to go back to work. The union pleaded with her not to go in. The lads pleaded with her as well. But she was determined to go. She had her mortgage to pay, she said, and could not manage without working. How did she think we were managing? We were all at our wits end.

We now had more police than ever drafted in. We stood with the pickets every morning, waiting for her to come through the village. She always had a police car in front of and behind her own car, so there was never any hope of being able to stop her, and try and persuade her to think again. The pickets used to shout 'scabby Pauline', at her. I will say this though, the girl did have guts going through the men like that. I could not have done that to save my life, let alone my mortgage. For months Pauline put up with this. Not one day did she back down. I often wondered what her thoughts really were. Did she ever regret it when she passed the picket line? She never did get transferred after the strike. She still works at Arkwright pit.

We women decided that what was now needed was a little diversion from the pressures of the strike. We all agreed that we would have a rock-and-roll disco. We could make some refreshments, have a raffle and make it a night to remember. Once again, Lady Luck was on our side. The morning of the disco, a reporter from the *Morning Star* brought us a donation of food, including a lot of tinned meat, just handy to fill up the bread cobs with. We had managed to get the pork pies and sausage rolls cheap so everyone had a feast. I do not think there was anyone in the disco that night that did not enjoy themselves. The lads kept coming to us ladies, asking when the next disco would be. We told them the next one would be a Victory Dance. We were very confident of that at that time.

We now had three lads from our Strike Centre going to Liverpool fund-raising. They were Stuart, Mick, and Vic. Every week they would come back with some money that they had spent hours on the streets collecting. At times it must have been really hard work, but they never complained. I used to love going up to the club, on a Saturday afternoon, to spend an hour or two with them, while they told me all that had happened to them in the week. Mick used to tell me some wonderful stories about an old-aged pensioner called Bill. He never went out anywhere. Like so many old people, he had got into the state where it was easier to stay in. Bill heard about the miners' strike on the radio, and that some of the lads were coming to Liverpool to raise money for food. It was this that gave Bill the urge to go out onto the streets to find these lads. To me, Bill will always be a hero. He found the lads and put ten pounds in their bucket. Then every week after that, there was always five pounds for the miners. Bill is blind but, come rain or snow, he would always be there, with encouraging words and money. We came to think of Bill as a part of our family. The children thought of him as Grandad Bill. Never will I forget the very first letter that I wrote to Bill, thanking him for all the love and support that he had shown towards the lads, and all our miners'

24

families. He took the letter with him to church, and asked the vicar to read it out to him and all the congregation.

Mick told me about it, when he came back from Liverpool that week. His eyes were full of tears as he told me, so of course that got me going as well. I felt myself filling up with emotion, just to think that Grandad Bill wanted to share this letter with others.

Then there is another very good friend of mine, also from Liverpool, named Brian Bolger. Brian is a retired teacher who during the strike, and after, gave all his time, energy, and love willingly, to help us in our fight for jobs. Brian is very highly thought of by the lads. He was always there when anything went wrong. He was their leaning post. I have had some really inspiring letters from Brian, praising what we were trying to achieve. I still write to Brian, and class him as a very dear friend. In fact, thanks to the strike, I have found a lot of dear friends, also travelled to places I would not normally have visited. I can honestly say that it made me more aware of things that were happening in the world. I no longer wanted to hide away, and sit and cry all day. Here was a challenge, and by God, I would see it through to the finish, win or lose.

Never will I take anything for granted again. All this time, I have been praying for Mr Scargill to give in. I just did not realize what issues were at stake. We are proud people. We will fight for the right to work. We are proud of our pits. Have not our grandfathers, fathers, and now husbands and sons, fought long hard battles, to protect our pits? None of us will ever be the same again. We will show the world that we are human beings. We refuse to be the under-dogs, although our men have to be like worms burrowing under the earth. Do people realize just how much it ages our men? They get old before their time. Conditions are terrible. For people who have never been down a pit, I advise you, if you ever get a chance to go down, please do. After I went down, I wondered why the men ever wanted to fight to save them. I have never experienced anything as bad in all my life. Do you hear the men complain? No, all they ask is for the right to work, and a decent wage for a job well done. Surely that is not too much to ask for?

The children now broke up for the summer holidays. The council came up trumps again. They gave us a food parcel for each child receiving a free school dinner. We received one every week while they are out of school, and thanks to the extreme kindness of June and Bob, from our local fish and chip shop, our children got a free dinner every Wednesday. They had chips, sausage, and fish fingers, with either peas or baked beans. This is, as you know, the favourite food for children, so a lot of thought and love had gone into giving them this meal. Things like this must never be forgotten.

August 1984

Five months into the strike, it was now essential that we women from the Support Groups all congregate in the Women's Action Group, at its weekly Sunday night meetings. These were held mostly at the Union office in Chesterfield, at seven o'clock. Without these meetings we could not have survived. We were filled in with what was happening all over the country. We were given encouragement to carry on with our great fight. We were built up again. There were times when we were feeling very low. We tried to be strong for the men's sake, but it was very hard at times. We dare not let them see our depression. We must be their rock to lean on, their anchor. It was up to us to build up the men's spirits.

It was surprising what problems the men did come to us with. Mostly it was money worries. A lot could not cope with the situation. Savings were now gone. We advised them to get in touch with people they owed money to, and explain the situation. If you are fair with people, nine times out of ten, they are fair with you.

It was the young single lads that I felt most sorry for. They received nothing from anywhere to live on. All they got was their picketing money which, if they were lucky, would buy them a packet of cigarettes and a pint of beer. They lived with the constant fear of being dragged off the picket lines and arrested. How they always kept so cheerful, against all those odds, I will never know. We had three lads sent down to Lincoln Prison. Two were single; one was married with two young children. It was now up to us and the union to see that this young wife and family did not have to worry. We made sure a decent parcel was delivered to her house every week. We also sorted out clothes for her little ones from the sacks of clothes we had sent to us from wellwishers. Nothing could make up for her husband being taken away, but I would like to think that we helped her in a small way.

It was the second Sunday in August, when we were asked at our meeting if anyone was willing to go fund-raising in Great Yarmouth. We were being invited down by some ladies who had set up a Support Group to help us. Everyone went quiet. No one was in a hurry to say they were willing to go. There were more excuses than I thought possible. Most of them had young children at home, or could not spare anyone, because of the food parcels to be given out. Harriet nudged me, and said, 'Shall we go Norma?' 'Alright,' I replied. Had I really said that? That is always my undoing, being so impulsive. The times I have got carried away at meetings! Finally six of us said we would go, and it was decided that Harriet and I would go the second week. Now came the crunch. How would I tell Terry that I was leaving him to look after the children for a week, while I went off fund raising for our Chesterfield Centre?

Surprise, surprise, Terry took it better than I thought. If you want to go, he said, I will not try to talk you out of it.

I had at least a week to get organized. I had it all planned. I would give the house a good cleaning and do some baking. Yes, my family would be alright. The very next day, I got up early, raring to go. First I started on the bedrooms. There I was singing away, when I heard the phone ring. Calamity, it was Betty Heathfield. She was in a panic. The ladies who were going to Yarmouth this week had dropped out; she had managed to get two ladies from Duckmanton to go, but could Harriet and I help them out and go with them? I felt a moment of panic. I was not prepared. I arranged with Betty to phone her back. We only had an our to make up our minds, as the men who were already fund raising down at Great Yarmouth were to pick us up at eleven o'clock. So here I was, this Monday morning, running around like someone not quite right. Harriet

seemed happy to go. Terry was in a daze. I was panicking.
Would Terry and the children manage alright without me?
What clothes would I need? Why can't you ever find
things when you are in a hurry?

At last we were ready. I phoned Betty to confirm that
we were going. Terry carried our cases up to the club. All
the lads were joking with us about us going on our holidays. I knew that they were trying to cheer us up but just
this once I wished that they would shut up. My stomach
was churning over. I went into a sweat. What was I doing
here, waiting to go to the unknown? To make matters
worse, the lads did not arrive on time to pick us up. I
could not sit still; I kept pacing up and down; then the
phone rang. I ran to answer it. The Duckmanton ladies
were phoning to ask what was going on, they had been
waiting hours to be picked up, so naturally they were
furious. They agreed that the best thing for them to do
would be to get a lift down to us at the club, and wait with
us to get picked up. This would not take them long, as
their centre is only about two miles away from ours.

When the ladies arrived, there was still no sign of the
lads. We were phoning all over the place to find out what
had happened to them. Finally, they arrived in a broken
down old van. We were shocked when they opened up the
back doors for us to get in. There were no seats, just a
couple of boards across some crates. There were no side
windows at all. My heart sank at the thought of travelling
all that way inside it.

Terry took one look, then said, 'No way are you travelling in that thing; animals would travel better.'

I pretended that we would be fine. I dreaded him stopping us going, as we would be letting everyone down.
Three lads were taking us down, but no way were they
going to let us sit in the front. Those were their seats. (The
rotters.) Terrible was not the word for the journey. We
kept slipping off the planks; we twisted and turned until
our backs ached that much, we just did not know how to
sit. Our backsides were that numb, they felt red raw.

We arrived with mixed feelings, as the lads did nothing
but tease us on the way down. They had us convinced that
we would be stopping in a flat with them. There was no

way that I was going to put up with that. But relief, relief, they drove us to this Guest House. The welcome waiting for us was really fantastic. We could not have been better looked after if we'd tried. Harriet and I had a charming little room. We shared a bed, which we did not mind at all as, I will let you into a little secret, we both snore anyway. That night, the lady of the house, Betty, took us to meet their Support Group. I was nervous. People do not believe it, but I am really very shy until I get to know people. My friends might not agree with that statement, as they always push me forward at these times.

We were made to feel very welcome by four ladies, Betty, Barbara, Corrine, and Lynne. They realized that we were feeling a bit apprehensive about what we were in Great Yarmouth to do, which — putting it in a nut shell — was to go begging for money, food, and clothes. We had only been talking for about five minutes, when Corrine's husband came into the meeting to present us with a cheque for twenty-five pounds, from the Labour Party of Great Yarmouth. I cannot tell you how much this boosted our morale. Looking back, I now realize it was just as great a strain on these ladies as it was on us.

It was decided that we would go the following day leafletting. Betty would take us out the first day. With her husband being a Labour Councillor, Betty was used to going round doors, more so at election time. We were also invited to speak at a meeting the following night. I was even talked into doing this. I didn't like the idea, but if it meant getting funds, I was willing to give it a try.

That night I must have driven Harriet mad, as she had to put up with me going over and over my speech. It's just as well that Harriet has got a lot of patience.

The next morning we got up with mixed feelings. This was it. How would the people of Yarmouth take to us? Betty had a lovely breakfast waiting for us. I felt guilty eating it, knowing that my own family at home would be just having the toast, for their breakfast, without the marmalade. Betty stopped all morning with us leafletting, then we carried on on our own until tea-time. We must have travelled miles that day. When we finally got back to Betty's our legs were like lead, and our feet had blisters on top of blisters. Harriet and I crawled — and I mean crawled — up to our room; it was sheer agony. We must have looked a pretty sight. Talk about here's my backside coming! We can laugh about it now, but we could not then. We both flopped on the bed. 'Wake me in an hour,' I said to Harriet. We had to be ready to attend the Labour meeting two hours later.

What would I wear? I did not have very much choice, as all my clothes were now looking shabby, but never mind, I was sure that they would understand. Maybe they would even feel sorry for us, as I was now feeling very sorry for myself at the thought of the speech that was ahead of me. Betty and Lyn took us ladies to the meeting, which was held at the Labour Club. We had a drink downstairs while we waited for them to call us into the meeting, as they had to do all the minutes of the last meeting, etc., before I could do my talk. This waiting was the worst part. I had a Pils lager, to give me dutch-courage, as those stupid butterflies were chasing around my stomach. A gentleman came to escort us into the meeting, and I thought, this is it! My knees knocked together. The room was full of staring faces but wait, I heard a friendly voice saying, 'Please sit down, how nice of you all to join us tonight.' (Perhaps it would be alright after all.)

Now the chairman was speaking, 'These ladies are from Derbyshire. They would like to tell us how the miners' strike is affecting them and their families.' Harriet broke the ice by telling everyone who we were, and where we all lived. Then she turned to me and said, 'Norma would like to say a few words to you all.' Talk about panic, I just dried up. My mind was a complete blank. I took a deep breath. I knew there was no way that I could make a hash of it now. In my mind I could picture the lads' faces. They were all relying on us.

All my thoughts spilled out. I really let myself go. All our fears, pain, and hopes came tumbling out of my mouth. I just had to let them know that we were fighting for our survival. Not only was it our fight, but the fight of every decent person in Britain. If we went down, what hope had anyone else of surviving Maggie's slaughter of jobs. This was a battle that would go down in history, a battle of a lifetime, and if we were to go down, then we would do so fighting.

The whole room went quiet. You could have heard a pin drop. What had I said wrong? I could feel my face going red, but relief, everyone was now clapping. I had got through my first speech.

The chairman said, how essential it was to help the miners in their fight. They would collect jumble and toys for the children, as Christmas was coming up. Even if the dispute was over by then, families would still find it very hard to buy toys. Also they would try to raise money for us, with raffles, etc., and then everyone agreed to give us another cheque for twenty-five pounds that night. I felt a warm glow inside at the kindness of these people.

The next day we decided to knock on a few doors, as well as put leaflets through them. I really hated this part of it, so Harriet did most of the talking, while I just smiled in the background. At one house, the ladies were in the garden. They were all smiles until they realized that we were miners' wives; I could not believe my ears at the abuse that came out of their mouths. Tell your lazy good-for-nothing men to go back to work and feed their own brats. They all want putting in holes and shooting. I was really shocked. My first reaction was to run away from their taunts. I felt sick inside. It was my husband that they were talking about. True, they had a right to their opinion, but surely they could have put it better than that, without such cruel words. Here they were living in their snug little worlds. What did it matter to them that we were prepared to go on as long as it took, to safeguard our jobs and pits?

The two ladies from Duckmanton had been working in a different part of the town, but we bumped into them a little later. They were really depressed, as they had had a lot of abuse thrown at them as well. I gave them a good talking to. We had to take the good with the bad, I said. Just remember why we are here. Everyone is relying on us. It's a good job they did not know that I really felt like giving up as well, so I was trying to convince myself as much as the lasses.

When we told the ladies of Great Yarmouth what had happened they were very shocked. The area we were working was a safe Labour seat, so they had assumed that everyone would be sympathetic towards us. We felt better after we had discussed it with the ladies. It's funny isn't it, that a trouble shared is a trouble halved. A lot of good came out of the leafletting we did that week. Jumble, food, and a little money arrived at Barbara's house. Some was from old age pensioners. Barbara had one leaflet sent back to her house though. There was no name on it, but it was very abusive, telling her that it was a pity that she had nothing better to do than help the miners, when they were destroying the country. I was very worried about this, what if someone put Barbara's window through for helping us? Barbara said not to worry. She knew the risks when she got involved. I will never forget the love and kindness those ladies in Great Yarmouth showed towards us all.

By the middle of the week I was feeling very homesick, so I phoned home to see how they were all coping. Terry was missing me as much as I was missing him, but he reassured me that everyone was well, there had been no arrests, and the lads were in high spirits. I was very pleased about this, as I was feeling a little guilty, as with being so far away from the trouble, there were times when you were apt to forget, for a little while, the picket line struggle. It is your brain not wanting to remember. Then, when you go to bed at night, and think about your loved ones, it all comes flooding back, and you want to be back with them all.

We were to travel back early Friday dinner. The lads had a stall on the market. On the stall they sold miners' lamps, badges, pictures, and books. All the profits went to the Women's Action Group. The Council allowed them to pack up early, so as to miss all the heavy traffic. Never will I forget the journey back. We were now sitting on top of jumble, food, and toys, but I would have put up with anything to get back to my family.

Harriet and I went to the Women's Action Group meeting on the Sunday, to take the money that we had collected. They were very pleased with it, and asked us if we would go the following week, as no one else was available, and we now knew the ropes. We were very reluctant at first, but it was the same old story. We could not let anyone down . What a wrench it would be, leaving my family for yet another week. This second week, Peggy went to Gt Yarmouth with Harriet and myself. Peggy is a miner's wife from Heath. We were to stop at Barbara's house this time. Barbara is very good at organizing so we were well looked after. Her three children always made us feel at home. We decided that this week, as well as leafletting, we would go round all the hotels and public houses. A couple of the landlords were very abusive, and this hurt us a great deal, as they were classing all the miners alike. You will get the odd selfish ones in any industry. They told us that they had collected for the Kent miners that had been down at the beginning of the strike. The miners repayed them by spending most of the money on booze, then lying on the beach all afternoon. We did not want to believe this, but they would not be saying this if it were not true. I mentally cursed them for spoiling it for us genuine miners.

There is a hotel in Great Yarmouth called the Flaboro. I do not know what nationality they are, but I do know that they felt for us in our hour of need. Although the landlady was busy with customers, she still found time to welcome us, putting pounds in our collecting box, also giving us sacks of nearly new children's clothes. These people were true Christians. They made us feel like real people again, not like scum of the earth, as so many people made you feel at times. They gave us the faith to carry on, and made us feel wanted human beings once again.

After one very trying day, us lasses were feeling really physically and mentally sick. We felt dead on our feet. We spotted a lovely little church, and we decided to go in and rest awhile. We sat down and prayed. I will always feel that this was the most important prayer of my life. Never had I felt so close to God as at that moment. Tears were streaming down my face. Things were getting just too much for me. How much more could we take? I dared not look at Harriet and Peggy, in case they thought I was daft, but when I finally turned towards them, I was shocked to see that they had been crying too. But by gum, that cry must have done us all some good, as we took the rest of the week in our stride, and I believe that the people of Gt Yarmouth were getting used to having us around now.

September 1984

I was to do another two weeks in Great Yarmouth, but Harriet's husband refused to let her go any more. I was not surprised, as I could see how tired she was looking.

It was now left to Peggy and me to carry on. For our third week we stopped at Lyn's Guest House. We were given our own key so that we could come and go as we pleased. There was always a beautiful meal waiting for us at night, when we could watch television if we wished to, but as we usually had a lot of meetings to attend, there was not much time for relaxing. Most of these meetings were arranged beforehand, so we were prepared for them. Peggy did not mind speaking, which was a relief to me, as by this time I was beginning to feel the strain. I had my mind on home where things were getting very hectic. It was a struggle keeping the men solid; more and more were going back to work.

We used to go to meetings just outside Great Yarmouth at Lowestoft Labour Club. They were great to us there. We were always invited to pass our collection box round, even lads on the dole pledged their support to us. We were also told that if any Support Group would like to write to them, there would always be fifty pounds for them for food. They kept their word; they must have helped at least fifty groups. To raise this money these wonderful people used to risk prosecution. They went on to the streets with collecting buckets, and handed out leaflets about our cause. We heard later that one gentleman had been repeatedly warned by police, but he insisted on carrying on. How could we ever let people like this down? They were our inspiration.

We were invited to spend a little time on the picket line at a local hospital at Gt Yarmouth, where we were only too pleased to join with NUPE cleaners fighting against privatisation. It was a freezing cold day, but we stood a long time. The television cameras came, also the police, as they had heard that some miners would be supporting the cleaners. I do not know if they expected a bus load of us or not, but I think they got a shock when there was only Peggy and me and two of the lads that took us down to Yarmouth every week. I am pleased to say that the police did not stay long, as their presence always seemed to unnerve me.

That night while we were having our evening meal we watched ourselves on the television. At last we were getting into people's homes. They could not fail to know that we were in Gt Yarmouth now, and that we were aware of the fact that there was not only our battle to be fought, but many others. It always comes back to the same thing, the fight for job survival.

The fourth week that Peggy and I went to Gt Yarmouth was to be our last. We stopped with a lovely couple called Carol and Brian in their charming house right next to huge stretches of sand dune and the sea. Brian took us for a walk to the bottom of their garden to have a look. It was a beautiful evening. The sky was a very deep blue with little white clouds, like wispy cotton wool, moving gently across it. The sun was just settling down in the horizon, like a huge orange ball, its rays dancing across the sea. It looked just as if millions of sparkling diamonds were twinkling upon it. You could see miles all around. How peaceful it was! If only Terry could have been with me to share this wonderful scene, so calm and serene, a far cry from the picket lines.

Towards the end of the week, I was feeling right under the weather, as my asthma was playing me up, but Carol and Brian were great. They made Peggy and me relax a bit more. We had worked that hard for the month we were in Gt Yarmouth that it was now showing on us. Our minds were still active, but our bodies were worn out. When we got home this last week, we were told that no more ladies would be going back down to Gt Yarmouth, as there was not the money there sufficient for our needs — which ran to thousands, not hundreds. I did not feel very happy about this after all the hard work — and love — that these wonderful people had put into helping us all, but there was nothing we could do about it, as we had no money to go on our own. All I could do was to write to them all, explaining it was not possible for us to come down any more, and thanking them for standing behind us in our hour of need. The lads continued going down, so we were not cut off from them completely.

It seemed very strange now being at the Strike Centre every day, but like they say, a change is as good as a rest. One morning we heard of another trip for the children. This time it was for Blackpool. Once again, the children's names had to go in a hat. This time sixteen from our centre could go, along with two adults. Jonathan's name was lucky enough to come out, but as Shaun had gone to France, I dropped out of going and Ann and Una went instead. The people of Blackpool gave them a wonderful day. A lot of famous stars were there to entertain the children, among them stars from *Hi De Hi!* The papers were full of the good time the miners' children had. A heartfelt thank you to everyone involved in making such a lot of children and adults very happy. Many ladies from different Support Groups have written poems about that day. I know the memory of it will remain with everyone for a long time to come.

Nearly every year, most of the families in Arkwright go to Skegness Holiday Camp, but during the strike, we all had to cancel our holidays. So it came as a lovely surprise when our union men said they would raise some funds for us ladies to take the children to Skegness at the end of the season. I do not know who was more excited — us or the children. The union raffled off a beautiful Miners' Centenary Plate, which was won by someone in one of the surrounding villages. We could not have wished for a better day for our holiday. Even the sun was shining for us. Our children were very excited and all our pickets

came to wave them off. One of the local firms in Chesterfield had donated pop, crisps and sweets for the children,
which we were very grateful for, as their eyes lit up when
we gave them out.

When we arrived at Skegness Camp, most of the children went to the swimming baths, while Ann and I went
to see the manager. He was very charming to us and
insisted that we have a glass of sherry with him. He was
very interested in our Women's Support Group, and said
that he hoped that we would all have a lovely day. He had
arranged for us to have a fish and chip tea later on. This
was very good of him, as he knew that we were hoping to
have it on tick, as we had only raised enough money for
the bus. Before we were allowed to leave the manager's
office, we had to have another sherry (not that we needed
any persuading). We both felt a little tiddly as we rejoined
the other ladies. 'You have been a long time,' they said to
us. We started to laugh, and told them we had been
having a little tipple with the manager. 'We might have
guessed that was what you were doing,' they said. 'Trust
you two to be where the drink is,' but like I said to them,
jealousy will get you nowhere.

We all had a lovely day, the only trouble was that it
passed too quickly. Everyone felt tired out on the way
back home, but we found the energy to have a good sing-
song. The kids had the time of their lives. I only wish that
Maggie Thatcher could have seen their happy faces, and
heard the songs that they were singing, all about her.
Somehow I do not think that she would have been
amused.

Some of our lads had been sent by the union to fund-
raise at Brightlingsea in Colchester. They really enjoyed
going there, as they were so well looked after by all our
supporters. Pam's husband Harry went down there for a
few weeks. He got to know the students at Essex Uni-
versity very well. They had some lovely chats together and
Harry explained to them what we ladies were doing to
help keep the strike together. You can imagine how
thrilled we were when one day Harry brought us a cheque
from the students for one hundred pounds. All the money
from Brightlingsea normally went down to our main

centre at Chesterfield, so this was an added bonus for us. As always, this money came at just the right time. Whatever happened we had to keep those food parcels going. Women and children were relying on us. We could not let them down.

We had one man who was diabetic, so we tried to get him special food whenever possible. Then we had young babies to cater for. They needed plenty of dried milk and strained baby foods, as well as disposable nappies. We certainly had a big burden on our shoulders, making sure everything was going smoothly.

October 1984

In October, the unrest began again. The nights were drawing in, and it was colder than ever on the picket lines. When the alarm goes off at five o'clock, you just feel like snuggling down again in the welcoming warmth of the bed covers, but then you think: we must not weaken, we must show the lads that we are there to back them up.

More and more lads huddled in little groups, whispering about how the strike was going. A lot of them were getting pressure from their wives at home, urging them to go back to work. They were testing the feelings of the other men, as no one was willing to be the first to cross that line. The union men had noticed the unrest, so they were now giving the men daily talks, encouraging them to stand firm. National negotiations were still breaking down. Mr Scargill was talking of us stopping out for at least a year. Surely we would not be able to last that long? It must have been a bit of codlum on his part, just to frighten them, at least I hoped so.

One day when we were very busy at the Strike Centre, making up parcels, a van load of vegetables arrived. Did we want them? we were asked. What a silly question! Round we trotted to the back of the club to help unload them. When the van doors were opened the smell made us jump back. The stench really made our noses twitch. I had to turn away as I could not stop heaving. There must have been a ton of potatoes, all going rotten. The lads had to tip out all the sacks onto the yard, so that we could sort them out. They helped us by taking skips of rotten potatoes away, I do not know where they took them, and I did not

40

want to know, as the smell made you feel sick. Every now and again your fingers went into the rotten parts. By the time we got them all sorted, washed, and into clean sacks, we were all shattered. Our backs did not belong to us, but the pain did. Are we crazy or what? The things that we were prepared to do just to get a meal on the table. I am just glad that no-one had a camera to take a picture of us then, or people would be saying that the miners were crazy.

I will never forget the day that the union decided to pay the men their picket money in the union offices. My husband, who was on night time picketing, was in the office, when the police chased a couple of men up there. The doors were quickly locked after them. Outside the police were trying to burst the doors down. Some were trying to get through the windows. Three of them were smashed in. Not content with that the police tried to tip the hut over, as it was only a small prefab type of hut. It was rocking very dangerously. What I did not know was that Jonathan had followed his dad so he saw everything that was happening. He knew his Dad was in the hut, so he was in tears. The police cursed him, and told him to get himself bloody home. How can children be expected to call the police friends, when they treat them like that?

Jonathan came running to me in the Strike Centre. He kept repeating that the police were going to hurt his Dad. I had to calm Jonathan down but all the time I wanted to rush down to the pit, and take all the police on. I felt that furious. Then one of the lads came in and said that everything was now quiet. The police had arrested one of the men after promising not to harm him, but we were to find out later that they did push him around, and to make matters worse, he was not guilty of the charge against him.

Evidently, while the afternoon shift were picketing, some coal lorries sneaked into the pit yard, with the intention of loading up with coal to take to the power stations. One of the lads threw a brick at the lorry. As long as the police got someone for the offence, they were not bothered who it was. The lad they picked out for it did not throw it; he just ran when the police charged into the pickets. This lad did know who had thrown the brick, but he would not split on his mates. I remember telling one of my married daughters about these clashes with the police, but she did not really want to talk about it. I have always brought my children up to respect the police, so it was very hard for her to understand how her own mother could change so much. What I had to get through to her was that the battle we were going through with the police was on different terms. It was something we could not avoid; we were bound to clash. I still honestly believe that the presence of the police caused more violence. I hate any form of violence, but at these times you can get carried away by the situation; it just happens.

I can understand how my daughter felt. This strike must have seemed very silly to her, just as it did to me at the beginning. I also know that it was a great worry to her seeing us having to struggle. It was a struggle — I am the first to admit that — but at the same time I have a lot of things to be grateful for. If it were not for the strike, I would have continued being just an ordinary housewife, waiting on the family hand and foot, not knowing any other kind of life. The strike certainly broadened my outlook on life. It made me more aware of my family. They were now even more precious to me, and I would have gone through hell and high water for them. It was really terrible at this time to hear of marriages breaking up. What suffering they must have gone through! Here is the man torn two ways; there's his wife urging him to go back to work. She is most likely out of her mind with worry about feeding her children, and all the bills mounting up, then there's the husband with the union urging him to stay out, and his mates to consider, as they are adamant that there is no turning back now.

Perhaps, if Terry and I had not reversed our roles, with him looking after the children and home, while I went all over the country fund-raising, or worked at the Strike Centre all day, we might have had that same situation. I am sure that if I had stayed at home, whittling and worrying, it would have got me down as well.

At the same time I do not sit in judgement on those lads who put their marriages first, as all people have different circumstances. When your marriage is worth fighting for, politics do not come into it; your family must come first. I know a lot of people will not agree with this statement, but it is my personal feeling, and I am only pleased that Terry and I were never to be put through that test. We were among the lucky ones, as we had a few friends who did go back to work, through pressures at home. To be fair, I should also point out at this stage that we had lads go back to work against their wives' wishes and this also caused problems between them.

We are very lucky in this village to have a really smashing milkman, whose name is Mick. Never did I know him to knock on any miner's door for money for all the duration of the strike, but you could stake your life on the milk always being there every morning on the windowsill. I always felt very guilty, whenever I had no money to pay Mick, but he just grinned and said, 'I do not know why you worry, as I don't; I know I will get it when you are back at work.' What can you say to that? Already he must be owed hundreds of pounds in outstanding bills, he is a milkman in a million, and he is ours!

Janet, our friend from Haversage, rang me up at the Strike Centre one day to invite us ladies to take all the school children in the village up to a cafe in Haversage for their dinner. All we had to do was to get them up there. We were all thrilled to bits about this. Some of the lads said, 'Do not worry about the transport, we will see to that.' We took the children up in a van and two cars. As I used to live up this way years ago, I was able to point out places of interest to the children. Derbyshire is famous for its beauty spots, and as we made our way up into the hills, it was really breathtaking. All the leaves on the trees had turned to bronze and gold, with the sun shining through the branches. I tried to show the children, through my eyes, that beauty is all around us if we take the trouble to look. We have not got very much money, but we do not need it to enjoy a lovely day out in the countryside.

When we arrived at the cafe, our friends came out to meet us. When we walked through the door, we could not believe it. There on the wall was a big sign which read,

'Bradwell and Haversage Labour Party Welcome Arkwright Town Children'. Even now I cannot think about this without wanting to cry.

The ladies soon had us settled down to a delicious three-course meal. The lady who owned the cafe explained to us that she had just celebrated her wedding anniversary, and thought that it would be a good idea if she had a raffle that night to raise funds to give our children a hot meal. Not many people would have gone to all that trouble. They even thought of inviting the reporter from the local paper to come and take pictures. This really made the children's day. One of the children gave a little speech to the ladies, thanking them for all their kindness, and presented them with a Miners' Centenary Book, and a badge. By now there was not one dry eye between us ladies.

November 1984

In November, with more fog and rain, it was getting harder on the picket lines, but no way could we let our lads down. We were never allowed to stand with the pickets as the police always made us stand at the opposite side of the road, then surrounded us with officers. Often we were joined by members of NUPE. They were a grand lot; they always joined in with us whenever we had a sing-song. The police hated you to sing, as they said that it incited the men, but I would like to think that it was because it was getting through to the police that we were a hundred per cent behind our men, and that we were helping to keep the strike going by supporting them.

It was heartbreaking now to see your friends dwindling into work, not going through their mates on the picket lines like men, but going in like caged animals on the scab buses. These buses had been fitted out with iron bars over all the windows, even the driver always wore a crash helmet. How degrading this must have been for the men, having to ride on one of these buses. Most of them covered their faces, so that you could not recognize them, but the union always got a list of the men's names by the end of the day.

The management at the pit had now put up a big notice on the board, informing you how many men had now returned to work. This was of course to put pressure on the men still out. But we knew that with the amount of men they had, they could not yet turn coal. Most of the key men needed to run the pit were still out on strike.

After picketing our own pit in the morning, it was then

45

time to go onto Markham Pit. We used to get a lift there with one of the lads that were going, but to be honest, they used to take us under protest, as Markham was known for trouble with the police. Hardly a day passed without an arrest. The very first time I went there I was shocked. The men were huddled together in a very muddy and puddly piece of land beside the road leading to the pit. The police had them completely surrounded and stood above them, shining big headlights on the pickets. This particular morning we were told that we could stand on the bank above them, on condition that we did not sing and incite the men. We scrambled up this very slippery bank and got covered in slime. It was bitterly cold standing there, waiting for the scab buses to appear, so what else could we do, to keep our spirits up, but have a little sing-song? Some of the lads enjoyed singing with us. Suddenly a scab bus was speeding round the corner, and all hell broke loose. The lads have a special noise that they make when they are going to push to break the police cordon, and stop the scab buses going through. What a push it was that day! I got really frightened. Two police nearly went under the wheels of the bus. You could hear them thud against the side of it. The men panicked, and rushed up the hill where we were standing. We ladies ran into the corn field behind us. The police chased the lads right to the top of it. I just could not bear to watch. I knew that the men would retaliate and the police would make arrests. Sure enough, the police arrested one of our Action Group ladies. They know who the important ones are, as they have lists. (I know this to be true as the police have bragged off about these lists to us to frighten us.) This was a big feather in their caps, to be able to demoralize this lady in front of us. The police tried to push her down this banking to stand with the men; it was obvious to everyone that they had picked her out, as they were completely ignoring us. They knew full well that she would resist them. It was awful not being able to go to her assistance, as she was dragged away by two policemen, with her clothes pulled half way up her back. I felt like screaming 'Stop it, oh please, stop it!' But we had been warned at meetings that in these circumstances, we would be on our own. We all knew the risks that we took every time we went on a picket line.

My stomach was really churning over afterwards. When the lads started moving away to go back home the police dived into the crowd, pulled two young lads out, and roughed them up on the way to the police van. I just could not believe my eyes. The cameras had been filming but they suddenly switched off when this was happening. Someone shouted, 'Get those cameras moving, let people really see what is happening.' But they just turned their backs on what was going on. This is what they call British justice.

On our way back to the car that would take us home to safety, we passed the van with our lady in. She was all alone with a policewoman guarding her. She looked really lost. It was no wonder really, as we all knew the degrading things that the police put you through when they got you to the cells. The policewomen would strip you, hoping to find something they could call a weapon. They treated you like a hardened criminal or like an animal to be pushed around.

We were all struggling now more than ever. The children needed a good hot meal in their stomachs. It was now a case of getting what you could to survive.

A few of us ladies from the village decided that we would go into the fields when it was dark to get a few potatoes. We set off like a comedy act, dressed in dark clothes, amid a lot of giggles; half way there, I suddenly saw someone walking behind the hedge, and turned to tell the lasses, but they had vanished. I panicked and ran as fast as I could until I caught up with them. I will not tell you what I said to them when we finally got our breath, and to top it all it was only a neighbour taking his dog for a walk. So us fearless ladies set off again, looking over our shoulders all the time. When we finally reached the field, we had to crawl under some barbed wire. I got stuck and had to be rescued by the others. Here was I crawling among the spuds, thinking about all the creepy crawly things lying in wait for me. 'Start digging with your hands,' someone whispered. All I could find was thistles. I had not got half a dozen potatoes when it was agreed that it was time to go. I was not arguing as I was petrified.

There were more shadows than I thought possible. Everyone was scared stiff and we all agreed, never would we go again. You should have seen my face when I got home and opened up my sack. I had about three decent potatoes. The rest were the green ones that they plant when setting the fields. That was judgement on me for stealing. From now on we would just have to put up with what we had got.

One morning one of the union men came into the Strike Centre to tell me that he had got a phone number from the union offices in Chesterfield for a school in London. They wanted to help the miners, so I rushed home to phone them straight away. I spoke to Colin Diamond, who was to become a dear friend. He said that he and his colleagues would love to help our village. Could they come down to meet us all the following week? We readily agreed.

We were sat in the Strike Centre waiting for them to arrive when a van pulled up outside with Colin and his friends. 'We have brought you food, clothes, and gifts to put away for the children for Christmas,' Colin said. When they started to unload the van and put the goods on the club stage, we just could not believe our eyes. Where on earth had everyone managed to sit on the way down from London? There was that much stuff, and if that was not enough there were also two cheques, one from the staff at Colin's school, the other from Netley English Language Centre (Ann Hallam, a worker there, had sent it with Colin) with all the staff's best wishes. Who says that there is not a God? I only know that every time we were desperate, a miracle happened.

I would like to give you another example of this. One day in the Strike Centre, some of the lads were telling us how worried they were about Christmas. Naturally, they loved their families and it upset them to think that they would not be having a proper Christmas. Already the NCB were urging the lads to go back to work by offering them a lump sum of £350. This was a big temptation to a lot of men. We called it bribery. They would be going back for a handful of silver, selling the rest of us out, just like a Judas. Of course, this was a worrying time. Everyone knows that Christmas is a special time in the life of a little

child. Father Christmas is magic, of course he would come
— even if I had to stay up all night writing begging letters
to every union I could think of. The children could not
help it that their Dads were torn between the fight for
their jobs and their families' happiness at Christmas. Even
if it killed me, I was determined that they would still have
their Christmas.

We had put a large whisky bottle on the bar at the
Strike Centre to collect money for the children's party.
Nearly everyone put their change in after buying their
drinks. One day Janet, her husband, and two children,
brought us some more food down from Haversage. Her
little boy spotted the bottle, and asked his mum what it
was for. When he was told, he said, 'Can we do something
to help the children Mum, to get some presents for them?'
'We will do a sponsored walk,' Janet decided. We ladies
were invited to go along too, so we thought we might as
well get someone to sponsor us as well, as we have a lot of
friends who are not miners. Next we had to get transport
to take us up to Haversage, which is in the hills. I phoned
up Julie Gains, who has a car hire firm in Chesterfield. She
had been marvellous to the miners throughout the strike;
she asked me if the van we wanted to hire was for the
miners, so I told her all about the sponsored walk. Julie
said we could have the van free of charge for the day. It
was kindness like that that always made me cry. (Just after
the strike finished, their firm went bankrupt; if only we
could have done something to help them!) Never will their
kindness be forgotten.

Thank goodness that it was a nice day when we went
up to Haversage. I was amazed just how many children
were going on the walk. There was even a baby sponsored
on his mother's back, and also two black children, who
were lovely, so friendly, bless them; then of course the
little tots with their mums and dads. What an eye opener
this was to us. All these wonderful people, willing to give
up a day to walk five miles so that our children could have
a Christmas too.

I had mixed feelings when we set off. We had our
young children with us as well. Would we last the walk
out, let alone the children? To my surprise, we were really

enjoying it. The scenery was beautiful, the fields stretched on and on as if forever, with stone walls dividing them. The only trouble was the footpaths were all sludgy. We kept slipping all the time, but we had a good laugh about it. Then we came to some stiles to climb over. I took one look and nearly died. How on earth was I going to get through? The lasses started to laugh at me, as they knew what I was thinking, as I am on the plump side. I turned sideways to squeeze through, and promptly got stuck. Even I was laughing at myself. I had one hand on my stomach pressing it in, and the other on my backside holding that in, and hey presto, I was through. We all stood there laughing until our sides hurt. I had about five stiles to tackle altogether. The girls thought it a right joke; I have still not lived it down even now. At last we arrived back at the village, all very tired, but very happy. We were given sandwiches and a cup of tea at the cafe owned by one of our supporters. We could not have been more looked after if we had tried. How do you ever find the words to say thank you? To me there were never enough words to say how I felt. Words did not seem enough. My heart was just overflowing with love for them all.

Altogether we raised £360 between us. It was a fantastic amount; another miracle had happened. This would be enough to buy each child a decent present, and go a long way towards a party for them. This news really boosted up the men's morale, but quite a few men fell to the Coal Board's temptation, and went back to work. It was a sad day for us, but how can you blame anyone? They must have come to the end of their tether. It is not for us to judge, although we did feel a little bitter at the time. Things must have seemed rosier on the other side to them, although we found out later that a lot of men regretted going back.

We saw on the TV that Russia sent us some food, but it was stuck in some warehouse at the port to be checked for contamination. We heard that some of it had to go back and we were wondering if this was another trick by Mrs Thatcher to stop food getting through to us. But she would not starve us out; we had too many friends for that. Soon enough we had a delivery of the Russian food: two big sacks of flour, some soap, and wash-powder.

What a job it was putting the flour into polythene bags. We put four cups full into every bag. It kept puffing up into your face and making you sneeze. We were literally covered in it, talk about flour graders, but what a laugh we had. It even made the lads laugh when they saw us, so it was well worth it to see a smile on their faces again. It was great to have soap and wash-powder in our parcels that week. At last someone had thought about our toilet needs. It's these little items for personal cleanliness that cost so much, you had to think twice before buying them. Food had to be the first priority every time.

When we went to the next Women's Action Group meeting, we were informed that the Piccadilly Theatre in London were putting on a show for the miners. The money was to go into the central funds. Betty Heathfield was to give an appeal speech, but only one lady from each centre could go to the show, as they wanted to make as much money as they could on the admission tickets. I was nominated to go from our centre, as no one else was bothered. We were to travel from Chesterfield by van. We all met at the Labour Club, where we waited ages for the van to arrive. We were beginning to get a bit worried, as we would be late getting to London if we did not set off soon. At last someone shouted, 'It's here now.' We all filed out to it, but one of the Women's Action Group said, 'I am not travelling in that,' — it turned out to be the same kind of van that we have been travelling down to Great Yarmouth in. It had been good enough for us, but not for them. We were in a right bustle then, trying to decide what to do. In the end we landed up going by train.

When we finally arrived, we all went to a cafe for a meal. Betty said she would pay the bill. It was just as well, as I was lucky if I had three pounds in my purse. While we were tucking in to the meal, a reporter came in and asked if he could take our photograph to print in the evening paper. First of all we were very careful to make sure he was who he said he was, as we had been tricked before — all reporters have not been genuine. After the meal we all went back to the theatre, where we were warmly greeted, then shown to our seats.

We were up on the balcony, so we had a first class view of the show, which was called 'Here We Go'. All the artists were appearing without a fee. The whole show was based around the strike. It could not have conveyed it better. It was so true to life, we really enjoyed it. In the interval, Betty got up to speak. It made us feel very proud as she stood up on the stage, delivering her speech. At the end of the show, all the support groups who had attended the show were invited up onto the stage, to sing a song that had been specially written for us ladies. The artists who wrote this song for us miners' wives sang it through first then invited us to sing the chorus with them. We all stood in a line holding hands singing this very moving chorus:

WE ARE WOMEN, WE ARE STRONG,
WE ARE FIGHTING FOR OUR LIVES,
SIDE BY SIDE WITH OUR MEN,
WHO WORK THE NATION'S MINES,
UNITED BY THE STRUGGLE, UNITED BY THE PAST,
AND IT'S HERE WE GO, HERE WE GO, WOMEN OF
THE WORKING CLASS.

The audience went wild while we were singing it, shouting for more, which we readily obliged, after which we got a standing ovation. One of the lady artists hugged me and said, 'Look at them all, that's for you ladies, you are the real stars of the show.' That really did make me cry, to think that a famous star had said that to us. Suddenly I felt so humble. Never could you measure such kindness.

December 1984

There was a lot of unrest again now in the Strike Centre. The lads were sitting around with long faces. We seemed to be getting nowhere fast. If only we knew something positive! But we did not get to know anything, unless we watched the news, and then it was so depressing, all the bragging about how many men were going into work, and giving up the fight. It was breaking our hearts, after we had all stood together for so long, that this was happening. Our morale was at its lowest ebb. It was beginning to get through even to us. We had to keep busy, to keep going, we knew that it would get even harder before it was finished. Surely we had endured enough! How much more was going to be asked of us?

Some of our friends from our village had now gone back to work. It was really terrible, with the scab vans coming into the village to pick them up, everyone peeping behind curtains, and round corners, watching each other. Who would be the next to go in? Even some of the men cried when they confided to us that they could not go on any longer, but it was not for us to judge them after ten months on strike. As far as they were concerned, they had given all they could. Some men can cope with pressure better than others.

But right or wrong, the problem still remained. It was causing a lot of ill feeling in the village. Gone was the feeling of togetherness; it was now a village with a big black cloud over it. Men walked about with lowered heads. Even on the picket lines we were now seeing a difference. Most of the fight seemed to have gone out of the men. None of the men were going to risk getting arrested, and being in prison for Christmas. Already two of our lads were in prison and would be there until January. We knew that they were trusting us ladies to see that their families were well looked after, but even that must have been small consolation to them, knowing for certain that they would be parted from their loved ones at Christmas, as that is what Christmas is all about. This would be one Christmas that they would never forget. There would be a few tears shed that day, without a shadow of doubt.

We were now busier than ever at the Strike Centre. As well as giving out the food parcels, we were also collecting all the children's names and ages. There must be no slip-ups. Every child must receive a present. Altogether we had nearly one hundred names on the list. Things were beginning to get me down again. I felt so worn out. I never seemed to be able to relax with my family for five minutes. There was so much to do, presents to buy, then to wrap, also baking for the party, and the buying in of all the food. On top of this we had to buy all the extra food for the food parcels. Our men must not suffer any more than they had to. Everyone that had supported us sent us extra money. All of it would be spent on the families. We would worry later about where the money would come from after Christmas to carry on with the food parcels.

One day I received a phone call from the Strike Centre, asking us ladies if we could go up there, as we had visitors from Southend-on-Sea. They had travelled down to Arkwright to bring us some Christmas Annuals for the children. We were all very excited as we made our way up to the club, as it was lovely to meet all these wonderful friends. Waiting to meet us were Alf, his wife, Jean, and a friend of theirs called Peter. How excited they were to meet us! They rushed to buy us a drink, which was very thoughtful of them, as we could not afford to buy one for ourselves. We could not thank them enough for the annuals. Alf explained that he worked at a printing firm, so had got them at a reduced price for us. We were a little disappointed when Alf and Jean asked us if we had received our Christmas card with a cheque in it. I said, no, not yet. Evidently, the union men had received it and not passed it on to us. This upset me very much, as I thought it was very thoughtless of them, as a card would have meant a lot to us at that time. We knew that Southend were sending cheques to the union, and that was fine by us ladies, as we knew that if we were really desperate, they would try to help us out. But we tried to be as independent as we could, as the union had enough on their plate at the moment, finding money to pay the pickets, and keep all the cars on the road, as without these we would be lost, as most of the men came from surrounding villages.

Jean told us that they did not realize that we had a Treasurer in our support group, but now they knew, she would have a word with Nigel, who sent the cheques on behalf of Southend Labour Party, to send them direct to me in future. The union did not seem to mind about these arrangements, so that was alright. It was essential that we worked together for the welfare of our men. Harry, who had been going down to Brightlingsea, also had a phone call to go to Fred and Jean's house, where he had been stopping, as they had a lot of brand new toys for the children. What a lovely selection there was! Our younger children would have some really lovely presents. There was a doll's pram and a computer game among the toys, but it would not have been fair to give these to any individual child, so it was decided to raffle them off, and put the money towards the children's party.

The biggest of our worries now were our single lads. With the pits shutting over Christmas there would be no need for picketing. Their only source of money would be cut off. The poor lads must have felt as if all the cards were stacked high against them. Something had to be done to help them. I decided to sit down and write dozens of letters to all our friends, begging them for money to relieve the lads' hardship. What a wonderful response I got! Everyone I wrote to was willing to help. The lads would get six pounds each, certainly not a fortune, but better than nothing.

We had our children's party a week before Christmas. What a wonderful feeling as the first of the children came into the Strike Centre. We ladies were all there to greet them with a paper hat, balloons, and a whistle. Mums and dads came with them, so it was like one big happy family. I knew at once that the party would be a great success, because for the first time in months, there was happiness in the air. We were now waiting for our guests of honour to arrive (a few of the children who went on the sponsored walk and made this Christmas party possible for our children). We all cheered and clapped when they walked in the door. I had to turn away as I had tears in my eyes, and a lump in my throat. They had made Father Christmas come true for all these children who were less fortunate than themselves. We had made a buffet tea, plenty of cream buns and trifles. The children were getting it down them as if there was no tomorrow. Then I told them that if they shouted loud enough, Father Christmas would come. It's a wonder the roof of the club did not come off, we made that much noise. Then in walked Santa Jack, with his sack of toys. The kids were jumping up and down with excitement, but we did not care. This was their day, as long as they enjoyed themselves, they could let all the village know.

At last Father Christmas got some sort of order. We helped him give the presents out. The look on their little faces as they received their gifts was a joy to watch. It is a moment I will always treasure. If only the whole world could have shared this moment which made me glad to be alive. The children got an assortment of presents, from dolls, teddy bears, watches, handbags, record vouchers, and of course every child received a Christmas annual and a game. But wait! There was a little girl shouting to Santa that she had not got a present. All the kids crowded round. They did not realize at first that it was Ann dressed up, freckles as well. The poor child did not get a present, but she did get a kiss off Santa, much to the delight of the children. Now it was time to have some games, which us ladies had to join in with. It was a great laugh, but we were all dead on our feet at the end. Already it was seven o'clock; the disco that we had hired had just arrived. While they were busy setting it up, we ladies went round giving all the children a big bag of sweets.

We all enjoyed the disco. There could not have been anything better to round off a really smashing day. There was not a sad face anywhere to be seen. I know that my heart was bursting with happiness; it did not seem to matter that my feet were killing me. What a day — and what wonderful people made it possible!

With the party out of the way, it was now time to think about the Christmas food parcels. We already knew that all the families on our list would be receiving a turkey, donated by a firm from Lowestoft, so all we had to concentrate on was a few extra fancy bits — and I do not mean that kind that our men would be happy with. One of the lads took Ann and myself down to Morrison's supermarket. We all went round with a trolley each. What a laugh we had. Some of the people could not believe their eyes as we loaded up the trolleys with one hundred and thirty jellies, biscuits, jars of beetroot, stuffing, and tins of fruit. Next we went down to Chesterfield market to buy some big bars of chocolate. I went up to the stall holder and said, 'Can I have one hundred and thirty bars of that chocolate, please.' He just stood there with his mouth open, then he started to laugh, then he spluttered, 'You are joking aren't you.' I at last convinced him that, no, I was not joking. As he was counting the chocolate out, he kept repeating, 'Never have I been asked for so many before.' I bet he for one was grateful for the miners' strike that day, as it boosted his sales.

The following day we received a message that the turkeys were on the way. The men who received parcels off us were told to come back to the Strike Centre after picketing to collect their turkey. There was an air of excitement about. We did not know what they would be like, big or small. After a couple of hours, the men were getting restless, so we rang up our centre in Chesterfield. Had they heard where the turkeys had got to? They did not know, but would try to find out for us. Hours passed. One of the men suggested that perhaps they were live birds, and had escaped on the motorway. We did not know what to think. We were getting as restless as the men. Then we had a phone call to say the lorry had broken down on the motorway. That's all we needed. Some of the men would have gone home there and then, but they wanted to be sure of a bird. We could not get them all in our freezers.

A cheer went up when they finally arrived at five o'clock, but what a performance giving them out! You ought to have seen them: they were massive. It took some doing putting them into carrier bags. We were frightened of dropping them on our feet, as they were very, very frozen. Needless to say the men were over the moon with them. Never in all our expectations did we ever think that they would be as big as they were. On Christmas morning we would be having a dinner fit for a king.

Here it was Christmas Eve. We had given the parcels out. Everyone was more than happy with them, although they would not get another one now until after the New Year. We had also shed a few tears with the young lads, when we gave them their money. (Bless them, I do hope that they had a good Christmas.) We decided that we would have a drink with George and Fay, our steward and stewardess, before we went home for a well-deserved rest. They too had worked so very hard during the strike. It was nice for all of us to sit quietly, having a little laugh at different things that had happened during the year. Suddenly one of the union men ran into the club. We could have some toys that have come from France, if we wanted them, he said. If we wanted them! Of course we did. So off he rushed to get some more cars to fetch them. We could only have got the strength from God that day to wrap all those presents. Our older children delivered the village children's presents, while we carried on wrapping the rest. Then convoys of cars took the rest to the other villages. This certainly would be a Christmas that would never be forgotten by a lot of people. Who can truthfully say that there is no Father Christmas now? I only hope that when these small children get older, their grandparents will tell them the story of how other people made sure that Santa came to even miners' children, even when their dads could not afford to pay him.

Christmas Day was here. Terry and I could not afford to buy each other a present, but what did that matter? We had each other, and that to us was worth more than any present we could ever buy. The children had their presents, we had food in the pantry. What more could anyone want, except, of course, for an end to the strike.

January 1985

It was the start of a new year, and still there was no solution to the pit strike in sight. I was beginning to think now that we had lost our battle. Pits all over the country were now producing coal. There was a general feeling among us that we had been let down. But we had come too far to give in. There was no way that we could return to work until out union leaders told us to go back.

Harriet and I still went down to the Women's Action Group meetings, down at Chesterfield. It was now more important than ever to find out what was happening. They had had leaflets printed, which we had to put in all the food parcels, telling the men that the strike was still alive in 1985:

Why? Because you have not allowed yourselves to be carried along on the wave of propaganda lies put out by the NCB and the media, submitting yourselves to the degradation of crossing picket lines and becoming a scab despite the hardships you and your family suffer.

I did not think that these leaflets would stop the men going back. Everything was now against us. But we were going to have one last bash at keeping the strike alive. We were going to walk from pit to pit until we had covered every one in Derbyshire. Betty Heathfield would lead us. The march started on a really terrible day. It was a right blizzard blowing but it did not dampen the ladies' enthusiasm. Hundreds of people came out of factories and shops to wave to them as they passed. Some even joined the march. Not everyone was against us! Even the TV cameras were braving the weather. So the march would be going into millions of homes that night, with the special message: You men that have deserted us and gone back to work, it's not too late for you to come back out and join us again, we can still win if we all stand together.

Of course I did not think for one moment that anyone would rally to the call. They had made up their minds. There would be no turning back. The march arrived at Arkwright two days later, on March 18th. It was still snowing heavily. Harriet and I were in the breakfast centre, making endless cups of tea for everybody, which was very gratefully received, as it helped to warm them up and keep them going. Then the march carried on to Chesterfield, where it finished with a rally the following day, which was Saturday. I suppose that in a way this march did help to keep our morale up a bit, but I still had my off days, as I am sure a lot more people did too. I was very lucky really, as I could go and talk to Paul whenever I felt really low. Paul is headmaster of our community school. He was so understanding, he let me babble on and on about all my troubles and fears. Deep down what I was really frightened of was that we too would have to give in, but the thought was killing us, how could we live with ourselves if we did? I remember that Paul always followed my line of thought, which made me think more clearly, and be able to reason things out a lot better.

Some of our lads used to go down to the docks at Hull to see if they could beg anything off the ships that were coming in. While they were there they were looked after like kings. The port stewards made sure that they were given a free breakfast, then the lads were told that if us ladies wrote to the port stewards at Hull, we could have three hundred pounds worth of food. All the lads had to do was go through to fetch it. We were really excited about this, as we could put extra food in the parcels, and God knows we could certainly do with it. Terry went with the lads to fetch the van full of food. It was a nice change for him, a change of scenery, away from the village and picket lines. All the food came to our house. I had to store it until food parcel day. What a performance it was! Our front room was so full of huge boxes, we could not stir in there. The lads were allowed to go to the supermarket and pick out everything themselves. What a wonderful selection they brought back. We could not have done better if we had gone ourselves. We thought that it was really kind of our friends in Hull.

I only wish that there could have been a happy ending to this, but it was not to be, as we were obliged to tell our main centre at Chesterfield about the food. It was only fair to do this, as they were still sending us food each week. It was decided that we could manage without a delivery from them that week, so of course our men did not get a bigger parcel than usual. But one thing they did get was a different variety of food, as the parcels were very much the same as a rule all the year round.

It was funny how things seemed to happen so unexpectedly. We had just handed out the last of the food parcels when we got a phone call from the ladies at North Wingfield. Would we like to go there for our dinner? What a question! We would be delighted to go. These ladies made a dinner for their men once a week, but this day they had prepared it all before they found out that most of the men had gone back to work. About twenty of us wanted to go, so the lads rallied round with their cars to take us there. North Wingfield is about three miles away from Arkwright. To help pay for the dinner, the ladies sold raffle tickets as you went into the centre. The winner was drawn out while you were having your dinner. The prize was a few groceries. I was lucky enough to win them one week. We had been going for our dinner for a couple of weeks when one of the ladies said that all their funds had gone. Unless they could get some more quickly, they were sorry but they would have to stop making any more dinners. They would be grateful for any suggestions to raise money. Here was my chance to help them for being so good to us all at Arkwright. I advised them to write to Hull about some food, also to Lowestoft, as they had promised to send fifty pounds to any centre in need.

The following week when we went for our dinner, the ladies were beaming all over their faces. Not only had our friends in Hull agreed to let them have some food, but they had actually brought it through to North Wingfield for them, so that they could meet the ladies, and tell them what a good job they were doing. The next good news was that Lowestoft had sent them a cheque, not for fifty pounds, but for one hundred pounds. We were overjoyed for them. Now the ladies could carry on for a few more weeks.

One morning when I got up, there was a letter from our friends in Southend. Jean and her husband Alf were writing to see if any of us ladies would like to spend a weekend with them. All expenses would be paid by the Labour Party at Southend. They thought that it would be a change for us, and besides it would also be an opportunity to meet all our Labour Party friends over there. Guess who was going? Harriet and I were once more nominated to go, but we did not mind, in fact, we were looking forward to it. We travelled down to Southend by train, and we were met at the other end by Jean and Alf. At once we felt so at ease, as if we had known them for years. That evening, Jean had made arrangements for all the people involved in supporting us to come round to meet Harriet and myself. You should have seen the mouth-watering buffet that Jean and Alf had prepared. I had nearly forgotten food like that existed any more. We met such a lot of people that night, among them was Nigel and his charming wife Angie. I had so much looked forward to meeting them, as Nigel had been writing to me and sending us cheques for some time now. Nigel presented us with a cheque that night and I felt a lovely glow inside, as you could tell that it was being given to us with so much love.

Later that night, I had a joke with Harriet, pretending that it was up to her to say a few words of thanks to them all. Did I laugh at the expression on Harriet's face! She did not know whether to laugh or cry, so I quickly put her out of her agony, and said I would make the speech. What a difficult speech it was, as I think by now we all knew really that we had not a hope in hell of winning the strike. I told them that our strike was a family affair, that we were proud to have stood alongside our husbands. We had fought a long hard battle to try to preserve their jobs, and our sons' jobs in the future. We had the feeling now that we could not win, but by hell, when our men had to go finally through those pit gates, then us women would walk through with them, our heads held as high as we could get them. We might have lost, but our men would go back to work with dignity, knowing in their hearts that they had given all they could. Maggie can strip us of everything, but one thing she can never take away from us is our pride. That belongs to us. One day people would realize just what we were fighting for. Just wait until all Mr Scargill's forecasts come true. We have not gone through all this suffering for nothing. Let's hope that in the future a few lessons can be gained by it. Never can we let all we have gone through be in vain. I am sure that one day people will look back on the strike and say, the miners showed us the way. We too should fight for our rights with the same determination, strength, and guts. They will shut our pits, we know that, but no-one will ever be able to turn round and say that we did not put up a battle for them. We gave all we had to give, and we would do it again if we had to.

Everyone stood clapping with tears in their eyes. Nigel said that if it were possible, they would all be there to clap the men as they went back into work. By now it was getting very late and one by one people were leaving. Time seemed to go so very quickly. We were sorry to see them all go, as these were our friends. We needed them and their comforting words. When we went to bed that night, it was with a lighter heart, but in the back of our minds was the thought of the struggle still to come. Could we last out? This is something that only we had the answer to. This problem we had to face on our own.

The next day Jean and Alf took Harriet and myself sightseeing. Southend really is a lovely place. Everywhere was so peaceful. We stood at the top of the gardens and looked down on the sea. It's funny how the sea always gives you a feeling of serenity. For one crazy moment you can forget the stresses of the world. Little did we know just how much we still had to bear when we finally said goodbye to Jean and Alf later on that day. Even they knew that the next time we met it would be in such different circumstances. It would be the end of the strike one way or the other.

February 1985

February began with a sad day for us. The canteen ladies told the union that they were going back to work. What could we say? They had worked so very hard for nearly a year now, but they feared for their jobs now that most of the men were abandoning the strike.

The union men had a meeting with the ladies to try to coax them to give a little more thought about giving in, but they were adamant that they have given the strike all they could. Nothing would change their minds. What were we to do now? Already the days are getting colder, our men had now to go without a hot breakfast into them. There was an air of dejection everywhere. It was just like at the beginning of the strike again. All the lads sprawling about in the Strike Centre, like little lost souls. We were all beginning to feel as if we had been left high and dry. We were completely in the dark as to what was happening, not even the union men seemed to know what was going on. But the signs were plain to see, as more and more men were going into work.

But what could we do about it? Even we had to shove thoughts of going back to the depths of our minds. Everything looked lost. There was no hope of any more talks. We felt really deserted, as if no one cared what fate awaited us. I was told by one of the managers of the pit, that if the remaining men still out on strike did not go back soon, there would no longer be a job for them. I felt sick with worry, as Terry had thirty years of service behind him. He could not afford to lose his job, but already we had lost so very much, how could we give in now? I prayed each day that an end would come to our misery, as I knew that both Terry and I were getting to the end of our tether. There were now only four families still out on strike in our village, each one wondering when they too would have to give in. Surely we had suffered enough by now? Our minds were bogged down with worry. Little did we know that this month was to turn into a nightmare, the memory of which will linger with us for our lifetime.

Never will I forget the day that it happened. One by one the lads were strolling into the Strike Centre from off the picket lines, when one lad rushed in shouting that Tommy Lax had just collapsed outside the club with severe chest pains. We wanted Tommy to go to the hospital, but he pleaded, 'Please take me home.' So one of the lads took him home to North Wingfield, then called in the doctor, who told Tommy to rest, as he had had a slight heart attack. We were all very worried about Tommy. He was a workmate of Terry's, so we talked a lot about Tommy in our house that day, but with rest we were sure that he would be alright. Then came the news a couple of days later that Tommy had had another attack and died. I stood there stunned, then I went cold and started to tremble. It came into my mind that surely I was dreaming. I even pinched myself to make sure that it was in fact a reality. I just could not take it in. Why Tommy? He was such a good and gentle man; he had fought so hard alongside his mates for the right to work. Now, when he was in his prime of life, in his forties, this had to happen. Now Tommy would never know how the strike finished.

For the rest of that day, I just could not take it in. I kept wanting to blame the strike. Would Tommy still be alive if it were not for the strike? I could not find an answer to it. This is something that we will never know, but one thing that I do know is that at that moment I felt very, very bitter. Then suddenly it came to me that feeling like this would not help Pearl, Tommy's wife. Her life was now in ruins. Already she had lost a great deal; now she had lost her most precious love, her husband. My heart ached for her. This pain only she could understand, only she could bear; we could surround her with love, but nothing could ease her heartache.

I was determined that Pearl would not have to worry about funeral expenses. We had friends all over the country. I was sure that they would rally round and help. I went straight home, sat down and wrote to all our friends, telling them about our Tommy. These letters were the hardest to find words for that I had ever written in all my life. I was writing them as if in a daze. It felt as if I was doing them in my sleep, then I felt the tears coming down my cheeks, and I woke up to the fact that it was reality.

Now came the day of Tommy's funeral. I had never seen anything like it before. All Tommy's mates were there, even those who had gone back to work. For them this must have taken some doing, going to the funeral, mixing with the lads that were still on strike; it certainly took some guts for them to go, but they were determined to be with their friend at the end. I do not think anyone could fault them for that.

All the men lined up each side of the avenue leading down to the church. A couple of us ladies were there to represent the Women's Support Group. We stood just outside the gates, waiting, each with our own thoughts and memories. The funeral procession stopped outside the church. Our friend Tommy had arrived. Pearl was in the car following Tommy's coffin. She tried to get out, but had to be helped. She was near collapse. She could not move. Now she cried uncontrollably. We were sobbing with her. Now I was praying as hard as I could, 'Please, God, help her to be brave.'

Then Tommy was gently carried past all his mates, who stood at attention with their heads bowed. What thoughts they had at that moment only they will know, but all thoughts of bitterness had to be put aside, as we were all gathering together in God's house. It was so very peaceful in there, you could sense it slowly taking over your mind. I felt for certain that Tommy was in a far happier place. Sitting there listening to the vicar made me feel a lot better. Already there was too much bitterness in the world without me adding to it.

After the service, we all filed out of the church to pay our last respects to Tommy. His battle was at an end, but we had to carry on with our fight. None of us stopped long at the graveside, as we realized that Pearl and her family needed their privacy for a little while. I was to see Pearl again, before the week was out, as I was swamped with sympathy letters and money for her. Not one person that I had written to failed to send anything. Our friends at Hull put on a concert to raise funds for Pearl. All the artists gave their services free. This is what I call love, doing all this for a perfect stranger. We, the Women's Support Group, organized a fund-raising disco. We did not put on a buffet this time as we wanted everything we took to be profit. Terry and I went up to take the money to Pearl's house. I was very pleased to see that she was trying to pull herself together. We sat for about an hour talking. I am sure that it helped her being able to talk about Tommy, but it also struck me that Pearl was very worried about what was to happen to us. Even in the midst of her sorrow, she still had the time to chat with us about our troubles, and to tell us that we would always be welcome in her home anytime. Pearl was overwhelmed with all the kindness of people. I do not think that she could take it in at first. Later she said to me, 'I never knew people could be so kind.' I only hope that in time her heartache will heal a little.

We were only making up about seventy parcels a week now. As I have already said, we only needed four in our village, the rest for families living on the outskirts. We knew that each week there would be even fewer parcels to make up, as the men were still drifting back to work. Even we did not know just how much longer we could last out, as with most of the men back at work, people whom we owed money to were no longer willing to wait for it. After a year who could blame them? The union had the fight of a life-time now, trying to keep their men out. If only we could have seen where we were going, it would have helped. We were now just living day by day, hoping against all the odds for a miracle to happen.

Harriet and I still went regularly to our meetings at Chesterfield, but even there, it was the same. No one knew what was expected of us anymore. Betty Heathfield gave us all a pep talk to try to keep us strong, but we could feel the tension in the room. What we really wanted was for someone to say to us, 'Do not worry, it will soon be over, the strike is coming to an end.' But we came away from that meeting feeling more bewildered than ever.

Terry and I were now under great pressure. Even our own children seemed against us. They were fed up with having to do without; they kept on at their Dad to go back to work. We could not blame them really, as all their friends were telling them that they were now getting little treats, as their fathers had gone back. They must have thought if our Dad loved us he would go back too. We tried to tell them that it was because we loved them that their Dad was still out on strike. If he went back now, not only would he be a traitor to himself, but also to all the thousands of people who had put their faith in us. It was a heavy cross to bear, but we would try to keep loyal to our union. The union brought us out, so we must try to wait for it to take us in again.

The Women's Action Group had bought a consignment of men's jeans and boots. They allotted so many to each centre. We were very disappointed that there were not enough to go round, so we had to put all the men's names in a draw for them. I was pleased to see that all the men got one or the other of them. Terry got a pair of jeans, which he was pleased about as he was all raggy breeches. I had a fight on my hands getting them off him later to get them washed. Chesterfield Centre were now sending us bacon and sausage to put in the parcels, as they had a bit of extra money, with fewer parcels to send out.

Money was very scarce again. We had used all our funds up at Christmas. We only had the money from our weekly raffle coming in now, and even that was getting less and less. Here I was whittling again; something had to be done about it; I could not let our lads down. Harriet and I were sat talking over a cup of tea, when I said to her, 'Harriet, how do you feel about us going for one more time fund-raising, instead of just sitting here moping. Money will not just come to us; we will have to go and raise it.'

Harriet agreed something would have to be done if we

wanted to carry on with our support group. Next we had to decide where to go. We both agreed that it would be rather nice if we could go to London, as we could then meet David Townsend, and thank him personally for the love and kindness that he had shown towards us all. Later that day I phoned David, explaining what we would like to do. Could he help us in any way? David thought it was a great idea. We could leave it to him to fix us up with contacts, and somewhere to stop.

We were to go at the weekend, and would be stopping with a friend of David's called Marita. She is a teacher and lives with her daughter Rosie in a charming terraced house, in South-east London. I felt a bit guilty leaving Terry again to look after the children, but I consoled myself with the thought that it would only be for the weekend, as we had to get back to make up the food parcels. There was only Fay, Harriet, and myself to do them now, although we could always rely on the lads to help us if ever we needed them. Marita phoned me up to say that she was really looking forward to us stopping with her and Rosie, and that she would come to the station to meet us. This is what was so wonderful about all the fantastic friends that we made during the strike. Nothing was too much trouble for them. Everyone was so willing to give up their time for us.

True to her word Marita met us at the station, then drove us through the rush hour traffic to her home. I mention the traffic because I was overwhelmed with the speed and bustle. It was a far cry from our quiet little roads. I was pleased when we finally arrived at Marita's home. We took to her straight away; she was so warm and friendly. In no time at all, there was a hot meal on the table for us, then we were shown to our room, which was lovely big bed-sitting room downstairs, where we could relax whenever we felt like it. Marita also gave us a key, so that we could come and go as we pleased. This never failed to touch me, how people were willing to trust us, as we were complete strangers really. Later on that night, David came round. It was lovely being able to meet him at long last. He was as charming as I knew he would be. David was to take us to meet a friend of his called Helen. She had got some tickets for us to see a play. We met Helen in the theatre foyer, and were put at ease straight away. She took charge of us, taking us up to the balcony to meet her sister and her daughter called Loveday. We were soon chatting away like old friends.

The play certainly was different from anything we had ever seen before: just four girls doing mime. I must admit that they did it really well, but it is something that you would have to get used to, as we never have plays like that in our part of the country.

After the play Helen and her sister suggested that perhaps we ought to go round to see if anyone would be willing to give us a donation. We were surprised just how kind everyone was to us; they chatted with us, as well as putting money in the pint pots that we took around. We collected over forty pounds that night, which was very encouraging, as it was only a small theatre.

Helen was to take us under her wing the following day, and what a wonderful day it turned out to be. We even visited a hospital that the Government wanted to close. It was such a shame, a beautiful building like that going to waste. I was very sorry to hear later that it was finally shut down, despite the struggle of dedicated people to keep it open.

Helen's daughter Loveday had invited us later to the Young Socialists' meeting. She said she would try and arrange it so that I could speak at it. What a friendly group they all were! It was a pleasure to sit with them, listening to all the different debates going on. Then Harriet and I were invited up on to the stage, so that I could deliver my speech. It was a very emotional speech. I put my heart and soul into it. All my feelings came out into the open. I could sense that the audience was with me, more so at the end of it, as we got a really good clap. Afterwards we were allowed to stand just inside the doors for a collection. Once more we did very well, but I did feel a little sorry for all these young people, as evidently they had been giving donations all day long to different organizations. They must have been broke at the end of the day. I know a lot of people pull the younger generation down, but to me that day they really showed that they do care what happens to people. They were great to us, and we will never forget it. There is a lot of compassion in the youngsters today, if only we have time to understand how they feel.

Helen had arranged to take us to a friend's party that night, so we just had time to go back to Marita's for a quick snack, then to get changed, before we were off again. On the way to the party, Helen explained that we were going to Kate's house. She was giving a party for some students who were stopping with her. It was their going away party, so Harriet and I felt very privileged to be invited. Kate met us at the door. Everyone was really charming. They took us into the lounge to meet all the guests. Harriet and I could really relax with them all. Everyone was so eager to listen to our plight, and offer words of comfort. Marion was most interested in all we told her. Marion is what I call a genuine person. She really did understand all that we had gone through.

We went down to the basement to eat. What a beautiful room it was, so very large, I could not believe it. I could do with a room like that in our house, as we only have pokey little rooms. The food made your mouth water. I tried a little of everything, but Harriet was more cautious, as she suffers a lot with indigestion. It certainly tasted as good as it looked, I even had seconds. We were very sorry when it was time to go, as we had enjoyed ourselves that much. Nobody knows what it is like to feel so secure among friends, then have to leave them, not knowing if you will ever meet them again. While you are with them, it's just as if they have wrapped a lovely warm cloak around you, and protected you from all the horrors of the outside world. Marion said she would see what she could do to help us, and would phone before we went back home.

Harriet and I were up very early the following day (Sunday), as we knew that we were having a big miners' rally in London that day. We were not going to it, as we were going to a luncheon party at David's, to meet our friends who had supported us during the strike, but I had made arrangements with Terry to meet him and our youngest son, Jonathan, in Hyde Park beside the black lamp-post, then go on to David's afterwards. David and Marita were taking me to Hyde Park, but first of all we took Harriet to David's house. Everyone there was very busy, but I had time to meet David's mum and dad, also Valerie, David's au pair girl. They all made us feel so very welcome, I really only had time to say hello, before we were off again, promising not to be long.

We had to get through some very heavy traffic before we reached Hyde Park. Already the park was filling up. David said he would drive around while Marita went with me to find Terry and Jonathan. First I had to find the black lamp-post. You have guessed it: there were lampposts all over the place! What a life, nothing runs smooth for me, and to cap it all, I could not see even one face that I knew. So I decided to give it up as a bad job. Poor David had been going around in circles but he was very upset that I had not managed to find Terry and Jonathan. We were just driving off when I spotted them going into the park. I shouted, but they did not hear me. It was no good going back into the park, as I would never have found them among all the crowd. But at least I had seen them, and knew that they had reached London safely.

When we got back to David's house, all the guests were arriving. Soon the house was ringing with happy laughter and chatter, as we all sat enjoying a buffet. It's no wonder that I was putting on weight fast. David had arranged a raffle, and the children had great fun selling the tickets. I believe that they collected about eight pounds, which was marvellous. Then came the big draw. The vicar won a bottle of wine. I won some coloured candles and, blow me, Harriet went and won a book. Surely it must have looked like a fiddle, but everyone agreed that it could not have been drawn better. Then the vicar insisted that we should have the wine as well. I could feel the tears pricking behind my eyelids again. Such kindness always made me fill up with emotion.

Now it was time for me to thank everyone for all they had done for us. I started off by telling them a little about what it was like for us at the beginning of the strike, and how we felt now, like lost souls wandering about in a wilderness, just existing, and battling on against all the odds, hoping for a miracle to happen. Perhaps we would lose, but there was one thing that we had won and that was the love and respect of thousands of people all over the world. When our men had to finally go through those pit gates it would be with their heads held high, pride in their hearts, and I am sure with just a hint of a tear in their eyes. Some of David's guests were teachers. They were very concerned about what was happening to us, as they too were on the brink of their own battle for a realistic pay rise.

Sue, one of the teachers, was very sweet to us as she left the party. She hugged Harriet and me, telling us not to worry, as we would always have their backing, and that she would try to get some of her colleagues to support us, although they were already committed to another pit. Unknown to us Marita had been going round all the guests collecting personal cheques for our support group. This was done on the quiet so as not to embarrass us. All too soon everyone started to drift away, after telling us to convey all their best wishes and love to the men and their families. Now it was time for David to take us back to Marita's house. He chose a different route back, so that we could take in some sightseeing. It seemed a perfect ending to a lovely day.

Nothing was planned for us to do that night, as we had been pretty hectic for the last two days. It was nice that we could relax in front of the TV, and put our feet up for a while. We eagerly waited for the news to come on, as it was sure to cover some of our miners' rally. What a shock we got. Here it was on the screen for all the world to see. Police on horseback, chasing defenceless women and children, while our men were trying to throw young children over the railings to safety. Surely their day out should not have ended like that.

I found myself saying out loud, 'No, don't do it. Leave them alone. Can't you see that the little children are terrified?' What nightmares must now be etched on their little minds! I wonder how those police involved would have felt if it was their wives and children who were being charged at?

I was now trembling inside. Were Terry and Jonathan safe? I had to spend a couple of agonizing hours before I could phone home to find out, as they would not have arrived back yet. I had a lump in my throat as I heard Terry's voice, but he said that they were both back safely. He told me that they were on the bus waiting for everyone else to get on when the trouble started. The police started in by pulling just one lad out of the crowd, then they stopped half of the procession entering Trafalgar Square, just as Arthur Scargill was delivering his speech. Jonathan was terrified, as people were pushing against their bus, and it felt as if it was going over. Terry said even he was feeling rather worried. I felt that relieved that they were alright, that I then had a little chinwag about him not being at the black lamp-post to meet me. He blamed the bus for arriving late, but I was that pleased that they were safe, I could not be mad with Terry for long.

I do not think that Harriet and I got very much sleep that night. It was a relief to see daylight creeping through the curtains. We just had this last day then we would be returning home. It's funny really, but it seems to get harder and harder every time I go away. I really miss my family. We did not do much this last day, as everyone was now back at work after the weekend. Harriet and I decided to just go out with the collecting box and see what happened. Just before we set off, we had two phone calls. One was from Sue telling us that she had spoken about us to her colleagues, and that they were very willing to send us a donation. We were thrilled to bits at the news. Then Marion rang us to say that she was getting in touch with some friends of hers in Canada, to see if they would adopt us. This was wonderful news. Our trip to London was more than worthwhile. It is times like these that you feel so helpless, as there is no way you can explain to all these wonderful people just how you feel. It is just as if someone had poured new life into you, and given you the will to fight on. Harriet and I went in a few shops, talking to people, then we got on a train to get to Fleet Street as we had been given an address that might be able to help us. We were to be disappointed, as our lads had already had a donation off them, a couple of weeks earlier, which we knew nothing about. But not to worry, thanks to all the wonderful people who were willing to give us their valuable time, the weekend had been well worthwhile. What an emotional time it was the next morning as we said goodbye to Marita. In just a weekend we had got very attached to her. It was lovely to get back home, to tell everyone what a good time we had had, and that we now had enough money to carry on a bit longer.

March 1985

Now we knew that there was no hope of winning this dispute. Mr MacGregor was completely ignoring us. He had even been to America on a visit. He was just content to sit back and let all the miners drift back to work, and they were just doing what he wanted them to do. Where did we go from here? Why did Mr Scargill not tell us that we had no hope and to go back to work? We are not daft, even we could see what was happening. We were now the minority. Even in our Strike Centre, most of the men were only giving it until the following Monday, then they were going in to work. I was so worried, we had been out a year this week. A full year, and still no nearer to a settlement. Here I was worrying myself sick again, but having to reassure everyone else that it would not be long before we would hear one way or the other what we had to do.

At last, on Sunday March the 3rd, Arthur Scargill and the others were to meet to decide what step to take next. We sat glued to the T V all day, just waiting for an announcement. It was a very historic moment when he finally said we had to go back to work. It felt a big relief, but at the same time a big let down. We had suffered in vain. Now the Coal Board could do what they liked with us. Arthur had gambled, and lost. We had not really been fighting the Coal Board; we had been fighting the Government. Mrs Thatcher was behind Mr MacGregor all the way. We had put up a good fight, one that I am sure even she will remember.

Harriet and I went down to our Women's Action Group that night. It was a very depressing meeting, as we all sat and watched the news on TV. Emotions were running very high as Betty Heathfield tried to talk to us all later. A lot of the ladies refused to accept that the strike was all over. We had wasted a full year. Now we were on our own to pick up the threads again. Everyone met up at the Strike Centre the following day. There was not one smile among us. Some of the lads were still being defiant. There was no way they were going into work. We were told that all the pits would be going back together the following day (Tuesday).

Later on in the day, two of the pit managers came to our Strike Centre with big grins all over their faces. They had slips of paper with all the men's names on, and what shift they had to go on. I watched them as they called out the names and handed out the papers. They were really enjoying themselves. My heart was bleeding for the men. They were being humiliated in their own Strike Centre, and there was nothing that they could do about it. All of a sudden, I saw one young lad turn away, looking very upset. Then it dawned on me that he had been sacked by the Coal Board for damaging their property. He did not know if he would ever get his job back, and here were the managers rubbing it in. I wanted to scream at them, 'Get out of our Strike Centre!' But I knew I would only make matters worse. This poor lad had to stand there and take it like a man. If his mother had been there, she would have been very proud of him.

Terry was on nights. I wanted to go through the gates with him that night, but he said this was one thing that he had to do alone. Only the men will ever know what thoughts they had as they walked down the hill, for their first shift for a year. We had watched some of the other pits going in on the TV. A lot of them had brass bands playing, with their banners held high. It was a very emotional sight. It fair made you proud to be one of those that had seen the strike through to the end. True, we had faltered many times, but with a lot of help we had come through it all in one piece. Never once did we have to eat grass, as predicted.

Even though we had lost, Arthur Scargill looked very proud as he led his men back to work. And so he should have done. We had put up a valiant fight. We had backed him all the way, even when we did not always agree with all his views. Poor Arthur, even that day things were to go wrong. There was a picket on the gate, so they had to march back the way that they had come. He would not pass a picket. How could he with the eyes of the world on him? But I understand that the men went in the next day.

Things were not going too well at our pit. There was a lot of unrest. The men who stuck the strike out were being made to feel the outcasts. It would take a long time for them to settle down, and time is something that we have not got. Our pit might shut any day, although they had given it two years. We decided to keep our support group going, as our aim was to try and get our community back to the friendly village that we all loved, before we were invaded by the Yorkshire pickets. We knew that it would not be easy, but we were willing to try. We were really lucky, as we had Paul to help us. Without him we would not have had a community centre, and a place to meet and get together again. Already, we had had a cheque from Sue and her colleagues in London, as well as written confirmation from Leo Panitch in Canada that they did not see any reason for not adopting our village, even though the strike had ended. The men would need help for months to come.

We realized just how privileged we were to have such wonderful friends in Canada, as we knew that in the long months to come, we would have to face many more hardships. But now we could face them knowing that we were not alone. We had dear friends behind us, rooting for us every step of the way.

I am pleased to say that the young lad that was sacked from our pit did get his job back. We did not know then what would happen in Nottingham. Would they stay true to the NUM, or would they try to break away from it? There was only one thing that could be said to them, and that was, stand up and be counted. We are proud of our NUM. Without a union to turn to whenever you are in trouble, you are lost. The union had never deserted us. We should not desert it. We needed it more than ever now.

March 6, 1985

The time was 6.30 a.m. I was waiting for Terry to get back from the nightshift at the pit. It was just like turning the clock back one year. Like then, I just could not settle, until I saw him walk through that door, safe and sound. Once again I heard Terry's key in the latch. Thank God, he had got through his first shift safely. I only had to look at Terry's face as he came through the door to know that things were not as they should be.

'What happened, Terry?' I asked. 'Has it been a rough shift?'

Terry explained that altogether fourteen men who had stayed out until the end of the strike went back to work on nights. The very first thing they were ordered to do was to report to the manager's office, where they were all informed that the strike was over, and that they were expected to work as normal. If they wanted to they could go to the stores for new boots and helmets.

Talk about those famous last words from the manager. That was a laugh, as he and his men must have been on different wavelengths. When our men arrived at the area in which they were to work, it was as if they were not there. They were just ignored. They were the ones who were made to feel guilty. Friends Terry had known for years were turning their backs on him. They just did not have the guts to speak. Perhaps if they had, Terry might not have answered them, who knows? But in my heart I really believe that he would have done, as I could tell that Terry was visibly shaken that morning. To think that these men were his mates, who had stood on the picket lines with Terry. They used to be friends who had willed each other on every inch of the way. On the picket lines, they had braved all kinds of weather, and opposition together. Side by side they had faced those months of hell, and for what? For it to end like this, bitterness on both sides?

Terry and I sat down that morning, and had a really long talk. I think it dawned on us both then that we had a long battle still on our hands, even now the strike was over. All the bitterness, pain, anger, and confusion still remained. It was not going to be easy. No way would it go away overnight. Now more than ever, we needed strength to carry on. The miners were divided. The unity in our pit and village had been destroyed. I was now under a terrible strain, as several of my friends' husbands had gone back to work, so I could hardly go to them with all my problems. As I have said before, I can not blame them for doing what they thought was right, it can not be easy even for them. Come what may, I could not let anything spoil our friendship. I just would not. We had shared many years of friendship before the strike. Nothing would change that. After all, had we not just come through the most testing year of our life together? I needed them then, and now. Of course we had all changed. No one could go through what we did, and not change. It is nothing that you can see with the eye, but changes are there alright, perhaps even we do not really know the full extent of what it did to us yet. All I know is, that I am now more aware of what is going on around me, and at the moment I do not like what I see.

One thing that the Women's Support Groups all agreed on was that the miners and their families should not suffer any more. While they waited for a fortnight before they got their first pay packet, we made sure that they all had a food parcel. Words could not be found to explain how gratefully these parcels were received. I shall never forget the heartbreak of receiving our first wage for a year. It should have been a day of rejoicing, but it was just one big headache. After all, who do you start to pay first. It is a pity money does not stretch. They say money is the root of all evil, don't they? Without it, there is despair and misery. You just do not know where to turn.

This was to be the testing time for all our marriages. I know people will be thinking that surely after coming through the strike together, a marriage could stand up to anything, but you see there was a big difference now. Everyone that had money owing them, wanted it now. Letters coming through the letter box had now taken on a sinister meaning. The message was very clear, pay up or else. Sometimes the strain was more than you could stand. It was enough to send you insane.

I was back to lying in bed at night, unable to sleep, thoughts just running around and around in my head. Sometimes I thought my head would burst with the strain. My poor brain was certainly taking some hammer. The only bit of comfort I could get was knowing that I was not going through this on my own. All miners were in the same boat. It was up to us to help each other, just like we had done in the past. Once again I now realised that I was living in a dream world. Our village had changed so very much. People dropped their eyes when they passed you, and did not answer when you spoke to them. I tried not to let it bother me, but deep down it hurt. God how it hurt. But you just could not let them see it. You still had your pride. I could see it was going to be a long drawn out struggle, up hill all the way, to get our village back to normal. Perhaps it would never really be the same again, which would be a great pity, as we have some grand people living here.

I had persuaded the ladies who dropped out of our Women's Support Group to rejoin, as I was sure that together we could work for the good of our community. It was up to us to carry on for as long as we were needed, with the main aim of bringing our community back to the happy village that it had been a year ago. Paul, the headmaster of our school, turned up trumps again, letting us put a notice in the school magazine asking people to get in touch with us if they needed help of any kind. If most of the miners' wives felt like I did now, they would be, I am sure, glad of all the help and advice that they could get. We were all in need of friends to get us over the next few weeks. During the strike, there seemed to be plenty of help and advice. Now suddenly we were left high and dry to get on with things on our own.

To be honest, I needed people to come to us, as much as they needed us. Talking to other people about your problems really does help. It is surprising what you can achieve by giving a little of your time, and a few kind words. I still personally believe that our Women's Action group in Chesterfield should have carried on helping the mining community for at least another year, as talking from experience I am sure that many of our friends would have been more than willing to carry on supporting us. They only needed to be asked.

As I have said earlier, we in Arkwright were very lucky and privileged to have the support of our friends in Canada. How thankful we were to be to them in the harsh months to come. Terry had only been back to work a few days when we had a load of coal delivered. Listening to the sound of it falling into our coal shed was just like listening to music. At last we could sit around a cheerful fire without the worry of where the fuel would come from to light it the following day. We had been digging coal out of anywhere that we could find it, knowing that if we had ever got caught, it would have meant prosecution, or even, for Terry, the sack from the pit.

Our eldest son, Andrew, had just left school. He wanted to work down the pit, so you can imagine how pleased he was when he received a letter from the training officer at Arkwright pit asking him to go for an interview on the 10th of April. I pray that Andrew will get set on, as there are no jobs around this area at all. People not working at the pit have to travel miles to their places of employment, so it costs them a fortune in fares before they can even start earning a living.

With such a lot of gloom about, it was a lovely surprise when I received a phone call from David Townsend in London. He was coming up to visit friends in Sheffield and, if it was alright with us, he would like to bring his family and friends to visit us for a day. We were thrilled to bits. Besides looking forward to seeing David again, we now could give to him the same hospitality as he had so kindly given to Harriet and myself. The thought of David coming to our home really bucked me up. It was just what

I needed to get me out of the rut that I was in, as at this time I was feeling very sorry for myself. Now I had hardly any time to think as I rushed around trying to brighten things up. Thank the Lord for the invention of paint and emulsion, as they really work wonders. In no time at all, the house looked a lot brighter. I really used to feel ashamed of how grubby everywhere looked, as for the last year we could not afford to decorate. After only a couple of months, the walls and ceilings get black with the smoke from the open fires.

Everything was well worth the effort, as we had a really super day with David and his two children, also with Hilary and her two children, with whom David was stopping for the week. We bought a video film for the children to watch, so that us grown-ups had a chance to sit and chat in comfort. It was a lovely feeling to be able to relax, and to talk to our friends about our many fears and problems. Just to be able to get things off your chest is a great relief, more so as people not in the mining industry can see things in a different light to us. Terry did not have time to organize a trip for David to go underground at the pit, but he did manage to take Hilary and David on a tour around the pit top, which they both enjoyed very much. I was sorry when the day had to end. It is always a sad time having to say goodbye to friends. The house seemed so empty afterwards, but I was thankful that we had shared the day together. I now had another memory to treasure.

On Saturday the 9th of March, we held the Women's International Day at Chesterfield. This was to be the first big rally to be held since the miners went back to work. Women had been working hard for months to get ready for the rally. It was a big privilege for us that it was being held in Chesterfield. Harriet and I would only be able to help out until twelve o'clock, as we had been invited to go to Liverpool for a get-together with other support groups on the same day. The sun actually shone for us that day, although it was still very cold. We stood about for a couple of hours with collecting boxes just inside Chesterfield football ground, where all the speeches were to take place. What a thrill it was watching all the buses arriving bringing our guests to the rally. Everyone kept coming up to us to have a chat. They were complete strangers, but within minutes, they were like friends, as we had so very much in common. We all wanted to do something with our lives, and to have a better world to live in.

I really enjoyed talking to some ladies from Greenham Common. Theirs must seem such a futile mission, but they stick it out, come what may. With just being there, it shows how concerned they are about the danger of missiles in our country. Later on in the morning, Harriet and I went down to the breakfast room, to see if they needed any help. Our ladies looked exhausted, but I was not surprised as they had been cooking breakfasts since six o'clock that morning for our guests that had come from as far afield as Scotland, and had been travelling all night. Harriet and I set to, clearing the tables and stacking the chairs. After this we were feeling shattered and ready for a welcome cup of tea. Then it was time for us to go to catch our train to Liverpool. We were to meet our hosts at a little tavern called 'The Flying Picket', but as usual we managed to get lost. Would you believe that even when we enquired at the local police station, they were not quite sure where it was? Finally down a little alleyway we found it.

Talk about a Liverpool welcome waiting for us! We were greeted by Pat Harvey and Lyn O'Sullivan, the two ladies who had organized this big get-together. Within seconds they had got us sat down with a big plate of food and a drink. We were treated like queens. Nothing was too much trouble for these ladies. They made sure that we felt at home. What a wonderful feeling it was for us, as people who had supported us came into the pub, and we were introduced to them. These people had given us so very much. They were our friends and we were theirs.

Later on we were put into a taxi, as the people who were putting us up for the night lived just out of town. We stayed with a young couple named Colette and Ray, who have just one little girl. At once they made us feel comfortable and at home with them. That is what stands out with everyone who has supported us miners. Nothing is too much trouble for them. We have always felt loved and protected. Ray came with us on the bus the next day. He was making sure that we did not lose our way again to the

'The Flying Picket', as we were all meeting there for lunch. Harriet and I had a lovely surprise when we got there, as Mick Whareham and his mum had travelled up to Liverpool, so as to support us, and thank our friends from Merseyside for all they had done for Mick during his fund-raising days.

Everyone was arriving now. The room was buzzing with voices and laughter. I was just content to sit back and watch. The air seemed to be electric with the warmth that everyone had for each other. We were all there for the same purpose of giving thanks to Liverpool. During the afternoon, all the support groups were invited to make a speech. It was lovely to listen to different experiences, and as everything was taped on video, our friends in Liverpool will always have a reminder of that day we all spent together. The highlight of the afternoon was meeting the guests of honour, Doreen and Mark Jones. You will remember that their son David died on the picket lines.

What struck me most about Doreen and Mark was how concerned they were for other people. They had lost a precious son, but in their grief they still had plenty of compassion left for others. Our troubles were still their troubles. They had written a book on David's life. Harriet and I bought one, and asked Doreen if she could write a few words in it for us, which she willingly did. I wanted a dedication in the book for my husband Terry, so you can imagine how it brought the tears to my eyes when I read what Doreen wrote: 'To Terry, may you be as proud of your wife as she is of you.'

Lunch was a very grand affair, the spread that was laid on for us was fit for a king. It must have taken hours to prepare. There were chicken legs, spare ribs, every cold meat you could think of, salads, pies, sausage rolls, different tit-bits on cocktail sticks, also the most mouth-watering gateaux you have ever seen. The ladies had really done us proud. We showed them how good it was as we all tucked in. Diets went out of fashion that day. All too soon the afternoon had slipped away. It was time to say goodbye to our friends. We did not know if we would ever meet again, but I do hope we will one day.

Harriet and I travelled back home with Mick and his mum in their car, but we were all very quiet, each of us with our own thoughts and memories. I was thinking how different things would have been if I had not become so involved with our support group. As you will remember at the beginning of the strike, I was dead against it. We at Arkwright already knew that our pit was to close, and the men had voted against a strike. Friends have told me since that they were having bets with each other that Terry would go into work first. In actual fact, he was the last to go back. It's funny really how this strike has affected my life. Before I was just content to be a housewife, but now I cannot settle down again to that boredom. I want to be out doing more interesting things. Gone are the days when I was tied to the kitchen sink.

April 1985

Andrew went for his interview and did very well. Now is the waiting time until the training officer gets the word that he can send a few lads to the training centre. Andrew has been told that there are nearly a hundred lads who have applied for a job at the pit, but only a very small percentage will be offered one. None of them may be set on, as there is so much uncertainty about the future of the coal industry now. That is why we miners must never lose sight of what our cause was all about: our pits that we have fought so very hard to save. All we want out of life is the chance to work, not only for our men, but for our children too. There is blood and tears spilt in those mines, but it is work. We are just ordinary folk, like every one else; we are not the hard-hearted bullies that some people try to make out. The only difference is that our men have rough hands and get very dirty.

I know that a lot of people seriously believe that the strike was a battle between Mr Scargill and Mrs Thatcher. Who knows? Perhaps they did have their private war, but make no mistake about it, there was no way that we were taking on a government. Perhaps it would be true to say that the government took us on, but in our hearts and minds there could only be one thought, that of our livelihood, and those of our children after us. To us that is how the strike started and finished. Who would have dreamed, over twelve months ago, just how this strike would have affected the villages over all the mining areas. There are ill feelings everywhere. There was a big question mark hanging over our pit. It could close any day, so there was a general feeling of unease. We had known for over a year that it was to close, but it is the uncertainty that gets people down. Already people were putting up their houses for sale. Signs were springing up all over the village. Where would it all end? In front of our very eyes, our village was slowly dying. Yet how could you condemn those families who want to get out?

How often I asked myself the same question: what future is there for our village now? Even I realized that our village would never be quite the same again. But surely we should not just give up? Where was our fighting spirit, our village was still worth fighting for. At all costs we had to carry on our efforts, to try and bring about the unity we once all shared. It was very hard trying to speak to people. No one seemed very interested. Many of them had had all the fight knocked out of them. Most of them had already lost so very much, their friends, hopes, and their ambitions. That was why it was so important now for us to find strength to carry on our fight. In our own back-yards, thank God, we still had some very good friends, willing us on, if only for their sakes we must not give in. We knew that it would be hard work, with all the unhappiness and despair around us, but we must try to keep going, *we must.*

I often sit and think about all the miners and their families who are still suffering. There are those who are imprisoned and those who were sacked. These men have no hope whatsoever to cling on to. Thank goodness money is getting through to their families. Their welfare will always weigh heavy on my mind. After all, it could so very easily have been me in that position.

What a pleasant surprise I had when I answered our front door one day to a gentleman whom I had never seen before. He asked me if I was Norma Dolby.

'Yes,' I replied.

'I am a friend of Leo's from Canada,' he said. 'My name is Ian. I thought that I would look you up, as I am over here on holiday.'

I was so excited. I made Ian a cup of tea and while he was drinking it, I ran to tell our support group ladies that he was here. We spent a very happy hour with him. I wish

Ian could have stopped longer, but he was on his way to Sheffield, where he had friends. Ian did take some photos of us to take back to Canada with him. I believe he even took some of our village and of the pit. Before he left us, Ian asked me if I would write an article about our village and our problems, and he would try to get it published in a widely-read magazine in Canada, as this might bring in more funds. True to his word, Ian did get it published for us, and sent us a couple of copies. The article that I wrote looked really grand on the letters page.

At last we had one cry for help, in response to our advert in the school magazine, but I never thought that it would come from my next door neighbour, Mrs Shawcross. Her Aunt Lizzy, who lived with her, had been taken ill, and is now bedridden. It is getting too much for Mrs Shawcross to keep lifting Lizzy to make her comfortable. Harriet and I were only too happy to help out. Lizzy was a grand old lady, but a bit grumpy at times. She would not think twice at telling you to leave her alone, when you were trying to change her, but we soon learnt how to coax her. In the end Lizzy used to look for us coming. I shall never forget how she used to pretend that she was asleep, but we could see her peeping under her eyelids, to see if we had gone. I have had many a laugh about this. It was as if the cheeky little madame was saying to us: get lost, I have had enough. But I could not blame Lizzy, not wanting to be messed about, as she was so very frail, just hanging on to life by a thin line. It was terrible having to watch her fade away, this poor very frail human being, just lying there in bed, watching the walls and ceiling all the time, and mumbling about her friends in the past. It was just as if she was waiting for them to come for her. In the end I found myself looking with her. It was heartbreaking. I prayed that Lizzy would not have to linger too long, as now it was a case of just existing.

It soon became clear to us all that Lizzy would be better off in hospital. There was nothing more that we could do for her. Harriet and I went to see her in hospital and I would like to think that she did recognize us, although all she was interested in was the fact that she did not have her earrings. She asked would I go and buy her some, from you know where, that nice shop. She died a couple of days later. Harriet and I felt very moved, as Mrs Shawcross sent us both a bowl of beautiful flowers, with love from Lizzy. Excepting for Mrs Shawcross, Lizzy had no close family, so only five of us went to her cremation: Mrs Shawcross, her two sons, Harriet and myself. One of Mrs Shawcross's sons is an ordained minister, so he conducted the service. I like to think that Lizzy would have liked that.

Terry came home from work with the news that the men were going on a token twenty-four strike to support some mates who had had their money stopped for a shift, because they refused to go back down the pit after bringing an injured man out on a stretcher. Evidently if you have worked half a shift you need not go back down. These men had done five minutes more than half a shift, but the manager said they would not get paid if they did not go back down. Of course I was pleased that the men were standing up for their rights, but at the same time I felt a bit fed up, as it could not have happened at a worse time, when we all needed the money to get on top of our bills. There is a happy ending to this story, as the men who had brought the injured man out did finally get their shift paid to them. And the injured man got away with no more than some damage to his ankle.

I think the men realized that the management could do what they liked with them now. It would be a long time before there would be trust on both sides. Our men had only been back at work one month when they were informed that NACODS were going on an overtime ban. This union is made up of skilled workers, for instance, men who do shot-firing, as well as deputies. Without them our men cannot work, so straight away their wages would be cut, and as it is the overtime that makes up a decent wage, our men were really worried. Low wages would not pay the bills that had accumulated since the last overtime ban and the strike. Once more we were all feeling rock bottom. The general feeling among the men now was: what does the future have to offer us? Have we gone through all this hell just to keep on suffering? Where will it all end? That's what gets to you most, the waiting to see what the final outcome will be.

May 1985

This month, we were very busy in the Women's Support Group. There was a never-ending stream of men coming to us for help. It was very hard not to become too involved in all the men's problems, as we had some terrible cases coming to us. There were times when I used to fill up with emotion. Their problems became mine. We coped the best way we could, but sometimes the money we gave them was just not enough. We had to be firm and give a set amount to each man, otherwise we could not have helped as many men as we did. One thing I am thankful for is the fact that we never let any of the lads down. We could not have done this without the help of our friends still backing us.

One typical case we had to deal with was a lad who was behind with his payments on a debt that he owed. He just did not know which way to turn. The bailiffs were going to take his parents' furniture in payment. He was at his wits end, but thank God, we were able to help him, and avoid his parents being shamed in front of their neighbours. Things like this should never be allowed to happen, but they do.

I believe that the biggest problem of all was lads that were behind with their rates. The Council had frozen them for the year the lads were on strike, but now they were demanding the two years' rates together, which was ridiculous. There was no way that the lads could find that amount of money straight away, not with all the other commitments they had as well. Even Terry and I were up to our necks in arrears. I can understand now just what it feels like when people are at their wits end and do not know where to turn for help. It is the last thing that you have on your mind at night, and the first thing on your mind in the morning.

Terry and I knew that it might not be long now before Terry got offered his redundancy,. It would solve a lot of our money problems, but in the meantime, we had to keep going. We decided to apply for a loan to tide us over. At the time it seemed the best way out of a nasty situation, but believe me, do not ever think of having a loan off a money lender if you can help it. In the end you pay at least twice as much back. We learned this lesson the hard way. These firms are getting rich on the poor. One thing that amazed me is the fact that not many more babies are being born to mining families this year. I would have thought that with all the leisure time that the lads had during the strike that more babies would have been born, just like there was during the power strikes a few years ago. I only know of one baby born, whose father works at our pit. It would be interesting to find out just how many children were actually conceived during the strike.

Harriet and I went on a weekend course to Northern College. This is a college for further education. We were going on a course especially for us miners' wives. This course was free if you did not have a job. It was just like old times, with Harriet and I sharing a bedroom. Most of the other ladies were also in the same block. It was very comforting to know that we were all together. Each block contained a little kitchen where we could make ourselves a cup of tea or coffee anytime during the night as well as toast and marmalade. All this was supplied by the college, which I thought was very good of them. Our main meals were eaten in the big dining room. It was just like one of those self-service cafes, where you queue with a tray, collect your meal, then go and sit down anywhere. The food was really good.

We had a busy program to get through that weekend, with short breaks in between. It's funny just how much you do not really know about your own industry. The courses were very enlightening. We ladies were all encouraged to talk a lot. Nothing different in that, I expect you are all thinking, but it was to encourage us to all have a say about each subject, as we all have different views.

The most interesting part of the course for me was learning how stories for newspapers are put together, and how different papers vary about the same story. We also learnt how to give a good interview for the television. I felt very self-conscious and nervous doing this, as the interviewer can ask you questions that can be twisted round to sound entirely different. Little did I know, at that time, just how useful this would be to me in the months ahead. All our nights were free to do what we liked. Most of us went for a drink at a little bar in the college grounds. To get to this we had to go underground through some cellars. It was only a little place, but very warm and cosy. We really let ourselves go, singing our strike songs. It was also an ideal time to get chatting to ladies in the other groups and to see what plans and achievements they had made since the strike. I was very sorry when the weekend came to a close, as it had all been great fun, despite the very busy schedule we had to get through. Our minds had been kept active, and most of all, everyone was encouraged to come out of her shell, voice her opinion, and this made the shy ladies come forward more instead of stopping in the background all the time. I felt very guilty again, as I had left Terry alone to look after the children. I wish there was somewhere for the men to go too, as at times they must have felt they wanted to unwind just like us ladies and discuss their problems with men trained to do just that.

Even our union men seemed to be keeping a very low profile. They did not have so much say at the pit now, not as if we had won the strike. It was not easy for them to carry on with their work, fighting on for the men's welfare and rights, but it was a job that they still had to do, even for the men who had gone back to the pit before the strike ended. After all they were still in the union, so still entitled to the union's help and advice.

I think it is fair to point out that a lot of men fell out with the situation because of personal problems. They felt compelled to give up, but that did not necessarily mean that they had fallen out with the union.

One of our union men asked the manager at the pit if a

party of us ladies could go down on a tour, as we had never been down a pit before. We were all very pleased when the trip was OK'd. There were six of us who wanted to go down, three of us from our Women's Support Group, Ann, Fay, and myself. It was a very cold morning when we all met outside the miners' welfare. We walked down to the pit together, amidst a lot of giggling. I think we all wanted to hide the fact that we were feeling a little nervous. First of all we had to report to the Training Officer, who would be looking after us. He was a really friendly man and quickly put us at ease. He told us his name was Roy, and after we had all signed our names, which is for safety reasons (so they know everyone who is down the pit, in case of a disaster), Roy told us the history of the pit, and how far the men have tunnelled since the pit was sunk in 1938. It was funny to think that the pit stretched for miles right under our village. It's no wonder that all the houses are suffering with subsidence and have big cracks appearing on walls and ceilings.

Now it was time to go and collect a helmet and safety gear, before setting off on our tour. We were all given a metal disc with a number on it, which we had to give in when we left the pit, so that they knew we had all come up safely. Arkwright pit is a drift mine, so you go down on what looks like a train (the men call it 'the cars'). Most of the other pits have cages which go straight down like lifts. With us being ladies the man letting us through the cars waived the rule of a body search. He said he would take our word that we had nothing like cigarettes, matches, or watches with batteries on us. Now we were all scrambling onto the cars, ready for our journey into the dark bowels of the earth. It was too late to say, 'Stop, I want to get off.' As we went down it was very cold. The air swirled around you. At times it took your breath. But it only took about twenty-five minutes to get to the coal face that we were going to. I was very surprised to see so much water down the pit. It was running all over making it very dangerous underfoot. We were slipping all over the place. Another danger was big girders. We had to shout 'girder' to the one behind us all the time. Even then Ann managed to bump her eye on one.

You would not believe that there are hills down the pit. Terry says they are everywhere and are called 'gradings', but they are certainly hills, as I found out walking up them. Talk about finding muscles that you never knew you had! At last, Roy said 'Here we are. This is the pit face.' It is a very narrow opening that you walk along. It is actually the floor of the roof supports that you are walking on. This face we were visiting was the best one in the pit, but even then we had to walk doubled up. If you forgot and tried to stand up straight, you bumped your head. How the men work the machines, bent over like that, I will never know, but these men on this face are supposed to be the lucky ones, as on some of the other faces you have to crawl along.

As we stumbled along the face, we saw one or two of the men. I did not recognize them until they spoke, they looked so different with their black faces in the light of your small lamp, fixed to a helmet. But it was grand to hear a friendly voice, when I felt so petrified. I was beginning to feel very claustrophobic. I felt as if I could not breathe. I turned round so that the air was blowing on my face and took some deep breaths. I dared not let the others see how I was feeling. I knew it was silly but all I could think of was: how will they get me out if I pass out? Would it be on the big conveyer belt that was to the side of us, taking the coal to the surface? If it was, then I hoped that they would switch off the powerful coal-cutter. It made me shiver just to look at it. Would we ever get to the end of the face? At last, Roy said, 'Crawl through those two little openings, and you are off the face.' I certainly do not recommend crawling either. It is very rough on your hands and knees, but it was worth it to feel not so confined, and to be able to stand up again. Once more there were friendly faces to greet us. It must have been a change for the men to see us down the pit. It broke the boredom for them a bit. It is a very funny feeling when you are coming out of the pit, as you have to go through some big steel doors that are called 'air doors'. You can feel your ears popping as you go through them. You have to be very careful as you pass as there is that much pressure behind them they really bang shut behind you.

Now we were waiting for the cars again. I was hoping to see Terry on one of them, but we were on the first set of cars, and Terry came on the second set, as he was working a long way from where we were. As we came out into daylight once more, we saw all the lads waiting to go down on the afternoon shift. I felt very sorry for them. But it is a job, isn't it? After we had stripped all the gear off, Roy took us to the canteen, for tea, sandwiches, and cakes. We had certainly been looked after, but it is an experience that I would not like to repeat.

I staggered up the hill on the way home, and could not wait to get into a hot bath. I was black bright and it takes some getting off. It even gets right up your nose, so goodness knows how much of it we had inhaled. People who think that miners are overpaid ought to do a shift themselves. I doubt very few of them would moan then. They deserve treble what they get.

June 1985

I had a phone call from David, who wanted my permission to give the letters I had written during the strike to a friend of his who was writing a book. I felt thrilled about it and readily gave my permission. Another surprise was that David had a friend who had been approached to write a play about the strike. Would it be alright, he asked, if Geoff Case, a playwright, came to visit us to talk to me and our Women's Support Group?

What an honour it was for us all to meet Geoff, and Gordon Fleming who was to direct the play. Instantly they put us at ease and we spent a pleasant afternoon trying to help them picture the strike through our eyes. When I look back on this strike, I realize that it was made up of *if only this had happened*. Geoff had the hard task of making up a play that was not biased. No way could he take sides, which must have been difficult for Geoff. But we in the coal industry had been through so very much, now was the time to try to get back the unity we once had before the strike.

At the beginning, we were all solid at our pit. We had one purpose: the saving of other pits. That purpose had not changed. We were still fighting for that. The only difference now was that every individual pit must fight for their own rights and to keep their pit open. But at the same time we must never lose sight of the fact that behind every miner is a family: these just have to come first, as without your family you could not carry on. After all, what is life without your loved ones? If you really love your man, you stand behind him, never mind what he decided to do. I have always believed that no job can compensate you for personal happiness. True, we are not all made alike. Some of us are not as strong as others. Don't let us condemn those who felt that they had to give in, just let us be pleased that we could understand them and carry on. They gave all they could. We should thank them for that, not go on condemning them for months of dedicated service to the union. Our union is our backbone at work, but equally important are the families that our men are glad to get back to at the end of a gruelling shift.

I can honestly say that I was so involved with the strike that even I was beginning to forget where my duties lay, but I do know now that if my husband had said to me, 'Follow me to the end of the earth,' I would have done. I cannot think of life without him. It is too painful. At the end of the day, we have all got to make up our minds where our priorities lie. I would like to think that mine are within the safety of our four walls, in our home with our family. All this I explained to Geoff and Gordon, who promised to keep us informed of their progress.

I told Geoff that I was attempting to write a book and he gave me a lot of encouragement and advice. I feel now that it is very important for people not to judge us so harshly. If I can prevent that then I will be happy. Our union organized a party for the lads who stopped out until the end of the strike. Our friends Colin and Barbara, from a school in London, were coming down for it, and I looked forward to seeing them again. The party was held at the next little village, called Calow, in their community centre, so as not to cause any more ill-feeling in our village. I must be honest here and say that I did not stay at the party very long, as a couple of weeks earlier I had had a disagreement with the union men at Arkwright pit. It was my personal way of showing them how we ladies felt. Terry, Harriet and I did go for an hour, as we could not spite the lads or our visitors. None of it was their fault. Barbara and I got all emotional when we saw each other. As we hugged each other, I only wished there could have been a happier ending to the strike. They had helped us so much.

Terry had come home from work with the news that

they were going to make many men redundant. He was hoping that he would get it soon, as he.says that it just is not the same at the pit now. It was the general feeling among the men that redundancy could not come soon enough.

I had a lovely letter from Brian, our teacher friend in Liverpool. He sent us ladies in the support group a very moving poem, which really made me fill up when I read it. Brian came through to Arkwright to meet us all. That is the good thing about this strike: all the wonderful friends we now have. You just cannot explain how it feels to be able to thank them in person for all their support. You feel full of pride in them for standing alongside you all the way. When you think about it, it must have been a bitter blow to all our supporters when we lost our battle.

At the Women's Action Group, they had a letter inviting forty-five children from the area to go on an adventure holiday to Denmark, paid for by the Danish Seamen's Union. All the children who wanted to go had to have their names drawn out of a hat. It was agreed that their fathers had to have stopped out until the end of the strike. My friend Una's lad, Steven, wanted to go and you can imagine how excited he was when his name was drawn out. Una now had a king-sized problem of how to fit Steven up with clothes for the trip, as that was the last thing any of us could afford at the moment. The bills had to come first. Luckily, we still had a little left in our funds, so we were able to help. Steven had a wonderful time and made a lot of friends in the fortnight that he was away. One lad still writes to him and hopes to be able to meet him again when he comes to England. When he comes we will do all we can to see that he has a lovely holiday too, so he can go back home with the same happy memories that Steven brought back.

It was now June the 18th. Exactly a year ago, a fierce battle was raging at Orgreave, where so much blood was shed during the strike. Police on horseback were running our men down. One woman was tending to an injured miner when a policeman on horseback aimed a baton at her head. Luckily she survived the onslaught. That day should be etched on everyone's minds. Was it just a coincidence that June 18th was also the anniversary of the Battle of Peterloo in 1819? Orgreave was a repeat of that fateful day when the armed forces trampled down men, women and even children. They, too, were gathered together to demand their democratic rights.

July 1985

We were determined to go to Skegness again this year, as we could not afford to go last year. All of us felt worn out with all the worry and strain of the past year and we were ready for a break. The problem that arose now, of course, was how would we be able to afford it? Terry went to the bank to get a loan so that I could at least get the children a decent set of clothes. We knew that it would not be long now before Terry got his redundancy, so we would be able to pay the bank back soon. Getting the loan was a great relief to my troubled mind. My nerves were all frayed.

How excited we all were while we were waiting for the bus to arrive to pick us up. (I should explain that we get free transport to take us to the camp.) The children laughed and chatted all the way to Skegness. I felt a lump in my throat just watching them. To think that some children never get a holiday. It should never happen in this day and age. All children love the seaside. It was going to be lovely just to have our meals put in front of us, and no washing up after. I was determined to really enjoy myself and get a good rest.

What a week it turned out to be. It rained bucketfuls every day. We could not believe it. It cost us more money as the children liked to play on the arcade machines all day when it was wet. We took them to the swimming baths and games' room whenever possible, but it was difficult to keep them amused all week. We spent hours playing cards with them. By the end of the week, I was fed up and ready to go back home. Even at the camp, the atmosphere was different this year. It did not seem the friendly place that it was before the strike. Everyone seemed to be watching everyone else, not wanting to be the first to speak. The camp seemed to be divided in two: those who went back to work, and those who did not. There is nothing worse in this world than hatred. It is like a rot that sets in.

When we arrived home I found a letter waiting for me, informing me that there was a bed waiting for me at hospital for the following week. This made me feel rock bottom, really depressed, although I was expecting it (I had already cancelled one appointment). Perhaps it was because I was run down, but I got it into my head that I would not survive this operation. I had convinced myself that history was repeating itself. Was it just a coincidence that Terry's first wife had done the same as me, cancelled her hospital bed to go on holiday, only to tragically die later on the operating table. I got myself into a right state, which was silly really, as when your time comes, it comes, doesn't it?

August 1985

Geoff Case came to see me again. He wanted a quiet little talk about the pit strike. It was lovely seeing him and I wished him every success with his play. Not very much more happened in August, except of course my operation. I will not bore you with all the little details. The main thing is that I am still here to tell my story. I think God must have spared me so that I can make you all bored to tears with this book.

I would like to say how very kind everyone was to me. The doctors and nurses were smashing and I had visitors galore. I could have set up a florist's shop with all the flowers I received. I did meet two ladies in hospital who were miners' wives, so we had plenty of time to chat about the strike and all its trials and tribulations. Even though we did not know each other at once there was a special bond between us. I had a lot of down days, but they always came over to my bed to cheer me up. One visitor that I did not expect was Paul. He had taken the time to come and see me after school. That is Paul all over, always thoughtful. I knew that I had to take it easy for a long while now, but the lads knew where I was if they ever needed me.

September 1985

After I had been lounging around for a couple of weeks, it was like a breath of fresh air when I received a letter from Leo in Canada saying he was coming over to England to attend the Labour Party conference. Could he come to visit us while he was in England? We were all so very excited at the thought of being able to meet Leo at last, we decided to give him a real Arkwright welcome. We would excel ourselves and have a party. Harriet and I went to the railway station to meet him, just like in the films. I was wearing our pit badges and a white carnation. I was also carrying a camera to take some snaps of Leo, but in the excitement I forgot to use it. Harriet and I were excited as the London train pulled in. Leo and I spotted each other straight away. What a wonderful feeling it was as we hugged each other. As it was such a special day, we had decided to have a taxi back to our house. Leo and I chatted as we drove to Arkwright, but we kept looking at each other, not quite really believing that we had met each other at last.

We had planned to take Leo on a tour around the village and pit top, but like all plans they did not quite come off. We had only been in the house a few minutes when the heavens opened. While we were waiting for the rain to clear, we sat with a cup of tea, having a very cosy chat about life at the pit and in the village. Then Terry had to open his big mouth and tell Leo about my book. I could have cheerfully strangled him, as Leo asked if he could look at it. I ought to explain that Leo is a teacher and a writer. What would he think of my puny effort? It was a relief when he read it and enjoyed it and told me I must carry on with it. This really bucked me up. To tell you the truth, I felt at times like giving the idea up, but Leo gave me the little extra push that I needed. He was also going to try to get me a publisher for it.

When Harriet came across to start on the tea, she was very surprised to see us all still in the house, as the original plan was for us to be out, so tea would be a surprise for Leo when he got back. Harriet and I persuaded Leo and Terry that if they did not go for a look around very soon, it would be too dark to see anything. I would have to stay behind with Harriet now to help her put everything out. We had just about finished when the men got back. They had not stayed out long, as it was raining bucketfuls once again. Leo's face was a picture when he saw the table all laid up. He really did look surprised that we had gone to all that trouble. But it was nothing compared to all Leo and our friends in Canada had done for us.

The ladies from our support group now started to arrive, so the next half hour was very hectic, with everyone getting to know each other. Leo was great. He soon put everyone at ease. Within minutes, we were like one happy family. The only trouble was that the time passed far too quickly, and the ladies left to get their own families their tea.

Later on Terry and I were going to the Labour Club in Chesterfield with Leo. He had made arrangements with Tony Benn to meet him there. Leo was to stay at a guest house with Tony that night, then they were to travel back to London together the next day. But first they were getting up early to go on the picket line at Scarsdale Hospital in support of the cleaners there, who were protesting against privatization. These firms are supposed to cut the costs of the cleaning, but what good is that when complaints are coming in all the time about dirty wards?

We all caught the bus to Chesterfield so that we could point out places of interest to Leo. I only wish his visit could have been longer so that we could have shown him all around Derbyshire, as it is one of the loveliest parts of Britain. As you go up into the Dales, it is really breathtaking. We were all very damp when we arrived at the Labour Club, but we soon got warm and spent a very relaxing hour chatting with all our friends at the Club. Geoff Poulter was there. He raised thousands of pounds during the strike for the miners at Bolsover pit. It must be remembered that the lads who were out there did not have to be, as it is in the Nottingham area, but they were supporting the NUM. With Geoff was our friend Mick Wareham, who used to chat to me for hours about everything that happened to the lads while they were fundraising in Liverpool. Mick is also at Bolsover pit and was helping Geoff get a campaign together to try and keep Bolsover in the NUM. They had a big fight on their hands, as Notts were voting to go 'Democratic' — they will be known as the UDM.

Geoff and Mick came over to talk to Leo to explain just how their campaign was working. They were sitting for hours under a little canvas shelter, talking to the men, and selling pit badges to raise money for the printing of posters, etc. The manager would not let them talk to the men inside the pit, but he could not stop them talking to them outside. Mick was telling us about an overman who told him to take off an N.U.M. badge he was wearing. Mick refused. I know just how strongly he feels about our union. He would sacrifice his job for it, but I hoped he did not do anything silly, as jobs do not come easy these days.

At last Tony Benn arrived. He looked very tired. He told us that he had just left a family party before travelling down from London, but he stopped with us long enough to have a chat and drink. I like Tony very much. He does not put on any airs and graces. When he is in your company, he is one of you. Now it was time for Leo and Tony to go. This was a sad moment for me. I said goodbye to Leo, not knowing when we would see him again. I hope it will not be too long.

October 1985

Terry came back from work today with the news that he had received a message while down the pit asking him to come up, as the union secretary wanted to see him. He was told to report to the Training Officer straight away about his redundancy. Terry was told just what he would receive for his 32 years service to the Coal Board. This consisted of a lump sum of money, a weekly allowance, and five loads of coal a year. Terry was given until the next day to think it over, but he had made up his mind months ago to take it, as he was far from happy at work. Some of the gaffers think that it is back to the days of slave labour; they are now the top dogs, and do they let the men know it.

I know a lot of men who went back to work early and were treated at first like heroes by the management. But it all changed after the strike was over. This was a big shock to them as I am sure a lot of them thought that they would always be in favour with the gaffers. As you can imagine, they felt very put out about it.

I was pleased that Geoff Case keep in touch with me. They had started producing the play, which was called 'Scab'. This title, I was sure, would have a big impact. I knew that this play would bring back a lot of unhappy memories to thousands of people. Although I realized that those who would be most upset would be the families of those still imprisoned and those who cannot get their jobs back, it was for their sakes that people should be reminded of the sacrifices our lads made to defend their right to work. These men must never be forgotten. We should think of them every day and keep on reminding other people that they, more than anyone, need all the support they can get. They are worthy of it.

I still believe that although we were fighting for the survival of our pits, we were made the scapegoats in the middle of a political battle against our union. This government did not want the likes of us to have a union to back us. We can be trodden into the ground for all they care. They know full well that the working class cannot afford the cost of fighting for their rights without a union. Only a union can fight for our right to a decent living, and decent working conditions. I have nothing but the highest regard for our union.

All our very many friends still kept in touch with me, so I was not really surprised when Marita phoned to ask if she could visit us with her daughter Rosie. They would like to stop a few days if it was possible. We were very pleased that Marita wanted to come to see us all. Now we could extend the same hospitality to Marita and Rosie as they had shown towards Harriet and me while we were fund raising in London. Marita and Rosie were to sleep at Harriet's, as there was more room there than at our house, but we would both share in making sure they had a good time. Marita was very interested in our little community school, so I took her and Rosie up to meet Paul. We toured all around the school, then stopped for lunch, which we all enjoyed very much (but then we always do, as Edna, our school cook, must be the best in Derbyshire).

The following day I was to go with Marita on a tour around the pit top. Roy, the safety officer at the pit, was kind enough to take us round. We found it very interesting as we did not realize just how much goes on on the pit top, as well as underground. They know exactly who enters the pit yard, and at the same time everything that is happening down the pit. That is one thing our pit is proud of: safety comes first. We have a very good record for this. It took us three hours to see everything, by which time I felt really exhausted. My operation was now telling on me, but it was all worthwhile, as Marita and I enjoyed every minute of it. When it was time to go home again, even Marita found it exhausting to walk up the hill from the pit.

Harriet had cooked a dinner which was ready for us when we came back.

Andrew had another letter from the pit saying how sorry they were, but they were not setting on any more young lads at the moment. He was very upset, as he had set his mind on getting a job in the coal industry. Now he had nothing to look forward to. Never mind how much he tries, he just cannot get a job anywhere. I saw a Coal Board van pass me today with a notice on the side of it saying: Coal is Going Places. It certainly is — to the dogs.

November 1985

Terry was now officially redundant. He had to go now every fortnight to sign on the dole, as did many of his workmates who finished at the same time. He received a letter from the Coal Board thanking him for all the years of service he had given to Arkwright pit. I think that we should have the letter framed as it is the only thing that the Coal Board ever gave him. There are no gold watches for our lads.

It seemed very strange having Terry at home all the time, but I was glad about it, as I always hated the thought of him being down the pit. I knew that there would be days when I would get fed up with Terry and Andrew under my feet all day, but in time I will get used to it. Retiring must be a very big step. I am sure boredom can soon creep in.

The Nottingham Coalfield had voted to go 'Democratic'. This was a sorry day for us all. The NUM still has thousands of loyal men at these pits, but like it or not, they are now in the UDM. Time will tell if this union will make a success of it or not, as they will not always have the government on their side. Even their pits will be on the hit-lists. It will be good to see how they will cope with that when the time comes.

I had a phone call from a lady called Jess. She wanted to come and interview me for a program they were making for Channel Four television. This program would be about what has happened to the support groups since the strike ended and how the communities were now coping with the situation. Betty Heathfield had told Jess that we still had a working support group in our village, and that is why Jess would like to do an interview. It was very exciting. Fancy me, just an ordinary housewife, going on the telly! Arkwright village will be flashed into thousands of homes. At last people will know that there is such a place. Perhaps I should explain here that in actual fact Arkwright is called *Arkwright Town*, just like in the movies. Years ago Arkwright was called the 'White City', as all the top half of the houses were whitewashed. Nowadays, most of the houses have sensible colours like dark brown or red, or are stone-cladded.

The day Jess arrived to start filming I was very nervous. Jess had brought two other ladies and a gentleman. They were all very kind to me, so that made me relax a little bit. While two of the ladies set up the lighting in the house, I was filmed walking down from our school. I tried to ignore the camera in front of me, but, believe me, it is very hard when you can see all the neighbours peeping behind their curtains, wondering what is going on. It took at least three hours to do the interview, but the time seemed to fly by, as it was all very interesting. I could not wait to see the finished program.

December 1985

It was nearly Christmas once more. What vivid pictures came into my mind about last Christmas, when we were so busy we wondered afterwards how we had coped. This Christmas would be very quiet in comparison, and for a lot of people, still a great struggle. Lots of children will be having even less this year and not only miners' children. Bless them, I hope Santa will not forget them completely.

I was very lucky with Terry getting his redundancy as I was able to buy my family and friends some nice presents without a lot of worry. I was determined to give them a good Christmas this year, as it was the last time that I could do it, with Terry now on the dole. How can I explain what it was really like when Christmas finally arrived? We had everything that makes for a good time, but it was just not the same. How could I enjoy it with the knowledge that so many of our men were still suffering and struggling? With the money from Canada we had helped all we could, but it was just not enough. Why has it always got to be like this? Some having everything, others nothing? It tears me in two just to think about it, but it is happening everywhere, and we are powerless to help everyone.

I spent hours looking up addresses so that I could send our good wishes to everyone that had supported us. This was a mammoth job, sending out all the cards, but believe me, every one I wrote was well worth it. They all brought back to me different memories, and made me feel very humble indeed. This is what Christmas is all about. Never will I forget the Christmas that we had while on strike. It will always symbolize the feeling of good will, just as it did when our Saviour was born, because if ever there was good will, then we found it with our friends that year. Our children became their children. Gifts were pouring in for them from all over the world. Never must it be forgotten, as long as we have the breath to tell our children, and their children after them, just how people took these children and us to their hearts. It was just as if they had wrapped a lovely warm cloak around us all, and told us that our suffering was theirs as well.

Most of all, we could not forget our men still in prison. We could not forget those who lost their lives during our dispute. At this time of good will, there would be no celebrating for their families. For them there would be tears and heartache. No one can take this grief away from them. This will always be their private hell on earth. How can we all know just what it feels like not to be able to say to them ever again, 'Happy Christmas', 'I love you.' We have to experience these things to know what they are really like.

The families and friends of our lads still in prison stood outside it on Christmas Eve, singing songs and carols. I guess that the lads shed a few tears knowing that their loved ones were near them at this time. Yes, I think a lot of tears would have been shed that day. Their grief is our grief.

January 1986

Terry and I went up to our Miner's welfare to see the New Year in with our friends, just as we do every year. I only hoped that it would bring a better year for us all. Marita and Rosie had come to stay with us again, so Marita would be going with us to the club to see the New Year in. What better beginning can we have than with a friend that has helped us so very much?

We always have a group or an artist on at the Club every weekend and at holiday times. We really got into the swing of things and danced the night away. By the time it got to midnight, we were all feeling very emotional. We all joined hands and sang our hearts out, many of us with tears streaming down our faces, as we remembered loved ones no longer with us and absent friends. As I turned to kiss Terry, I realised just how lucky I was. I am richer than a lot of people. I have the love of a good man. We have gone through hell together, but here we are still smiling, ready to face together whatever the future throws at us. At times it might be rough, but we will take it in our stride with the knowledge that our love will see us through.

We already knew that for a lot of men, this year would be a struggle, as some of them still had a long way to go yet before they would be out of debt. We are fighters. We might have taken a lot of knocks, but never mind how many times we are knocked down, believe me, we will just bounce back again. We are far from finished yet.

Andrew was excited, as the Career Centre have sent him for an interview for a job at a trophy-making place. Andrew loves artistic work, so although it is not very well paid, he is hoping that he will get set on. It also has the advantage of being in the next little village to ours, at Calow.

Andrew did well at the interview. Mr Wood wanted him to start the following Monday. You would think that, at last, Mother Luck was on our side, but no, we did not get away that easy. Evidently this job is part of a scheme. To qualify, you have to have been out of work for a year. Andrew still had six weeks to go, so the Career Centre slipped up. Luckily for Andrew, Mr Wood was willing to wait for him. It was a happy ending, especially as Andrew ended up loving his first job.

February 1986

At last, we saw Geoff and Gordon's play, 'Scab'. It was well worth waiting for. It lasted for ninety minutes and was about a striking miner called Brian Clarkson and his family, and the effects the strike had on their community and on his marriage. As the strike goes on longer and longer, he becomes very disillusioned with everything. Then, of course, the doubts begin to form in his mind whether or not the miners are standing firm for the right reasons, or is it political?

I know that a lot of people thought that the play did not show enough suffering, or the police brutality, but with the time allowed for it, it must have been difficult to fit everything in. Personally, I enjoyed the play very much and wish that they would do a follow-up of it. I taped it on the video, so that I could send it to our friends in Canada. But Leo wrote from there to say that they are unable to watch it, until it is converted to North America VHS speed. It's funny how you do not realize that videos are different in other countries. Brian, our teacher friend in Liverpool, also watched the play. He was very enthusiastic about it, and informed me that he would be showing it to his pupils in class. The subject would be: 'The Struggles of the Working Class'. It certainly was a struggle.

I shall always remember Geoff's words when he came to see us. He said, 'I only wish I had given more, now that I have met you all, and realize just how much you have suffered.' Yes, we suffered, but if other people can learn something from our mistakes, then it will not have been in

116

vain. Jess got in touch with me again, and told me that the video that they took of the support groups would be coming on Channel Four television in July, on the 'People to People' series.

It was just one year ago that our friend Tommy Lax died. I can still picture his funeral as if it was yesterday. To think that we have fought so damned hard to save our pits, and day by day you hear of another one being shut, and the terrible thing about it is that we have just got to sit back and watch it happen. There is nothing we can do about it.

At Arkwright pit, they were making a lot of men on the staff redundant now. There was a rumour that the pit would be shut by Christmas. This will certainly be a sorry day for us all. It will be as bad as losing a limb, as our pit is our village. We were still fighting hard to save our little village school, but it was getting to be a lost cause. It was just as if the village was being stripped of everything that was important to us. Arkwright is an ideal village for first-time buyers, as the houses around here only cost around £6,000 and the rates are fairly low. But it is common sense that young people will not want to settle around here if there is no provision for their children. It will mean the little ones travelling a couple of miles to the next village if the school closes. True, we only have twenty-three children at the school, but we have quite a few nearly ready to go there. I am sure that they could have a nursery there to cater for them, but of course it is the same old story: education cuts. We will battle on to the last to try to save our school, because it is so very important to our village that it stays open.

March 1986

Harriet and I went to a mass rally at Hyde Park to mark the first anniversary of the end of the strike. The purpose of this rally was to bring back to people's minds that, although the strike is over, the suffering still goes on. We have hundreds of lads still sacked and others in prison. Our pits are still under threat of closure. The NUM's assets are still being held. Thousands of jobs have been deliberately destroyed. This mass rally was organized by a newly formed organization called the National Justice For Mineworkers' Campaign.

Justice, such a little word that means so very much to all of us — the working class of Britain, regardless of colour or creed. Such terrible things are happening in our country today which should never be allowed to happen. Only we can put a stop to it. The voice of the people has got to be heard, loud and clear. We have been pushed around long enough. It is time we all stood up for our rights. Justice has to be done.

At the present time, we still have 520 sacked miners, whose only crime was to fight for their right to work. 130 of these men are from the Scottish pits. NO *JUSTICE*. Six of our men are still in prison through fighting for their jobs. I do sympathize with the family of the taxi driver, David Wilkie, who was caught up in the middle of our conflict. That tragedy should never have happened. I could never believe that the men found guilty of his death could have ever thought that it would end like it did, in a major disaster. Miners' families all over the country were shocked and stunned, as we listened to the news of this innocent man's death. Our thoughts were with both of their families. I only hope that in the future we can be forgiven a little for what happened that day, as in a way we are all guilty. We were all fighting for the same thing: survival. I do hope that the family of David will forgive me when I state that I think the sentences that our men received were too severe. When you think of some of the daft sentences dealt out to some people, our men who got eight years got NO *JUSTICE*.

We have all heard or seen on the television or in the papers how Arthur Scargill and his team went to court to apologize so they could get back their stolen NUM assets, which have been held by the Receiver. But have they been handed back? No. Is that *Justice*? We now come to the pit closures. We already know what the closing of our pit will bring about. Men are on the dole queue all over the country. The other areas will be affected the same. Already the industry has got rid of 35,000 men, a considerable workforce. Where will it all end? The young ones are no longer being set on at the pits. Twenty-four pits have been closed down. NO *JUSTICE*.

You can see now just how important this rally was to us all in the mining industry. We have got to remind people all the time. We cannot afford for one minute to let it slip people's minds. Since our dispute, more and more people have had to stick up for their rights. Thousands are losing their jobs through sticking up for them. We must not forget these people in their hour of need, as these people never let us down when we needed them. They backed us all the way. The hospital workers, the teachers, the print workers have all been involved in strikes. During our strike they sent thousands of pounds to help feed our families. We must make sure that we are first there, if ever they need help.

The message that we have now got to get across is that we want *JUSTICE*, and are willing to fight for it, at any price. We want a Britain that we can be proud of once again, not the rich getting richer and the poor getting poorer. We are fed up with all the police brutality that we still have with us. We want the friendly bobby days back again. Maybe those days are lost to us forever.

It is up to us to let the government know that we are fed up with all the orders that come from the top to the bottom. It's about time the orders came from the bottom to the top, as they should do. The voice of the people must be heard. Never mind the cost, we deserve this. It is our country, so we should have some say in happens to our lives. At the rally, we all had to stand in bitter cold winds to listen to the speeches, but it was well worth it. We all listened very intently to what we will have to face in the future. We still have a long way to go.

I had to smile at a chaplain who spoke, as he really got carried away, with the result that he swore. It made everyone laugh. I know now where the saying comes from — 'It's enough to make a vicar swear.' It was lovely to see Betty Heathfield there, as she had helped us so much through this strike. Her husband, Peter, gave us a very inspiring speech. One thing that he said lingers in my mind. A miner in Nottingham was sacked because he put up a notice on the noticeboard at the pit about an NUM meeting. I say this and always will, if they can sack a man for that, then they must be afraid of the NUM.

After the speeches, Harriet and I had a look around the park. It is surrounded by some beautiful buildings. It is like millionaires' row, but here in the park we saw a man asleep in a little pavilion, all haggard and dirty. He was lying on a bench covered by a car rug. What thoughts must this poor man have as he looks about him? He has not got much of a future. He must have to grovel about just like a dog. It should not happen anywhere, yet we hear of thousands just like this poor soul that have sunk as low as they can get. Perhaps he has resigned himself to this kind of life now, but for God's sake, he is a human being, with feelings. It should not be happening.

Seeing the thousands of people on the march must, I am sure, have shown people just how united we still are. Our union has not been destroyed, as intended by the government. It has withstood all that has been thrown at it, and has not been smashed to pieces, despite Mrs Thatcher's efforts. We finished the day off with a concert at the Albert Hall in aid of the sacked miners and for those in prison. Artists gave their services free. What a night it turned out to be! There were that many acts that they had to have their programs cut down. I wish I could remember all their names, as they all put their hearts and souls into it. Among those appearing were Tony Benn, Dennis Skinner, The Flying Pickets and Flaming Nerve.

Tony Benn brought the hall down when he got on to the stage to speak. It was our way of showing him how we all love and admire him. Tony really does share the troubles of the working class and he does something about it. That's why Tony and Dennis get so much written about them in the media. They say what they think. We need more men like them in parliament.

What can I say about Dennis Skinner? When he got onto the stage to sing, he had the crowd eating out of his hand. His first song was dedicated to all the many people who had befriended the miners. These people included gays and lesbians and all different nationalities, and the song was 'Let's Get Together'. I will say this, Dennis, you really do sing out of key, just like me, but we all loved it. It was so funny when you turned to the young lad who was accompanying you on the piano and said, 'Start playing after I have started singing.' We all thought that was great. Thanks for a most entertaining ten minutes, Dennis, and for everything else that you have done on our behalf.

Our bus had to leave London just after ten o'clock, so we did not see all of the show, which was disappointing. But we have happy memories of what we did see. I only wish that those people who are against us could have seen all the thousands of pounds that were handed over that night from different unions and organizations. We do not walk alone. We are not forgotten. We have gone through a traumatic time, but we have gone through it together, with pride. Yes, we still have our pride, and in the years to come our children will grow up with pride in their hearts that their forefathers were willing to fight for their rights to a job. Perhaps all the cards were stacked against us, but God knows we tried right to the end. At times the suffering was unbearable, but looking back it was all worth it, and I am sure I am speaking for most of the families when I say, if it happened again tomorrow, we would be out there again on the picket lines, fighting for *Justice*.

Since 1967, when redundancies were first introduced as a temporary scheme, more than 171,000 mineworkers have benefited by it. Now we have just heard that all redundancies in the coal industry will cease on March 28th, 1987. They should have ceased this month, but they have been extended for another year because of the time lost during the strike. This is a very worrying time for a lot of our men who are nearing fifty years old. It will be a toss up if all of them get it, and the majority of the men just cannot wait to get out of the industry. As one friend of ours has stated, 'I'm keeping my fingers crossed that I will get redundancy, as it just is not the same at the pit anymore. I just dread going every day. Our pit has changed so very much for the worse. The end of every shift cannot come fast enough.'

That statement is the very sad part of my story. After losing so much, men and their families are giving up. They just cannot wait to leave the pits. That is what the strike has done to so many of us. It has made us very bitter and ready to give in, but deep down I know that we should be strong and proud of how we came through the strike. This was the most testing time of our lives. Together we should look to the future and learn through our mistakes. True, we have not got a lot to look forward to, but we have to make the best of what we have. At least we still have got a roof over our heads, not like that poor man in the park, and of course millions like him. So let us be thankful for what we have, and be determined to do all we can to make this a better world to live in for other people less fortunate than ourselves.

What does the future hold for our village now? Only the years ahead will tell, but I know that I personally will battle on, helping people whenever I can. We cannot allow our village to die. We have heard that Paul is to leave us to become Head Teacher at Eckington. We will miss him a lot, not only for all he has done for our village in setting up a community centre, but most of all because he has become a dear and trusted friend, someone who we could confide in, with the knowledge that it would go no further. I know I will be joined by all the village when I say that we wish him and his family every happiness in the future.

We hope that he will come back to see us all now and again. Paul was our solid rock to lean on when we needed him most. He will be greatly missed. At this point I would like to say that Eckington is also a mining village that is now going through the same bitterness amongst the families as us. But I have heard that they have had it worse in their village than we have, as during the strike they suffered more violence in their village than we did. I know that they will benefit from Paul's understanding. When he finally leaves, part of us will go with him. Eckington's gain will be our loss.

It is up to us all now not to let Paul down. We must carry on where he has left off. This village of ours must live on. It is up to us to look forward to the future, making the best of what we have got. In our community centre, Paul has put up a photograph of the village with a rainbow over the top of it. I can never look at it without feeling very moved. Our village at the end of the rainbow — to me this is a sign of peace, and that is my dearest wish for us all. Please God help us all to find peace in our hearts and minds, so that with contentment, we can all face whatever the future holds.